25 CYCLE ROUTES

STIRLING
and the
TROSSACHS

D1424631

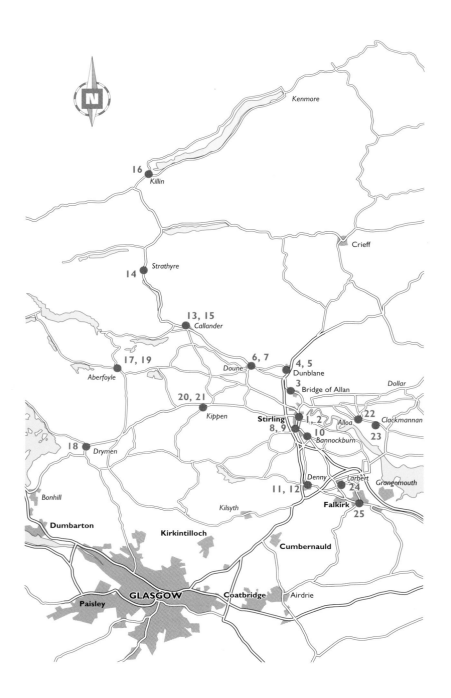

25 CYCLE ROUTES

STIRLING
and the
TROSSACHS

Erl B. Wilkie

With a Foreword by the CTC

EDINBURGH: THE STATIONERY OFFICE

Applications for reproduction should be made to The Stationery Office

Also available in this series:
25 Cycle Routes – Edinburgh and Lothian,
25 Cycle Routes In and Around Glasgow

Acknowledgements

The author wishes to thank Stirling Council, Environmental Services for the financial support given for the publication of this book and in particular Kate Smithson, Jim Towers and Ken McAlpine. Ken spent many hours checking the validity of each route.

The publisher acknowledges with thanks the support of Stirling Council, for their financial support and access to and use of transparencies used in this book. Also to the author who supplied most of the pictures used.

British Library Cataloguing in Publication Data

A catalogue record for this book is available from the British Library

ISBN 0 11 495821 1

CONTENTS

FOREWORD BY THE CTC

Cycling is healthy, environmentally -friendly – and above all fun! Travel at your own pace, meet people along the way and experience the real country. Explore parts of the country you didn't know existed – and improve your fitness at the same time! Cycling is good for you, so go by bike, and you'll feel a whole lot better for it.

Safety considerations and equipment needed

- Before you go cycling, check your your bike thoroughly for broken, worn and/or loose parts. In particular, check for worn tyres and broken/loose spokes. ensure that both brakes and the gear system are working well, with the chain lightly oiled and running smoothly. If in doubt your local bike shop will advise you further. Better to fix things now, than to spoil your ride later.

- Carry a cycle lock and key, and a small tool kit (spare inner tube, tyre levers, small adjustable spanner, puncture repair outfit, pump and Allen keys if your bike needs them).

- If you are really loading up for a big adventure your luggage should be on the bike not your back. A rear carrying rack is useful. Ideally pack everything in plastic bags inside a saddlebag or panniers properly secured to this rack. Check your load is balanced and the weight doesn't affect the steering/handling of the bike. If you prefer to travel light you can fit most things into a bumbag.

- Always carry food and water/liquid. Cyclists are advised to drink little and often.

- Comfortable clothing is essential. For colder days wear two or three layers you can take them off once you've warmed up and put them on if you cool off. Wet-weather gear is useful if

METRIC MEASUREMENTS

At the beginning of each walk, the distance is given in miles and kilometres. Within the text, all measurements are metric for simplicity (and indeed our Ordnance Survey maps are now all metric). However, it was felt that a conversion table might be useful to those readers who still tend to think in terms of miles.

The basic statistic to remember is that one kilometre is five-eighths of a mile. Half a mile is equivalent to 800 metres and a quarter-mile is 400 metres. Below that distance, yards and metres are little different in practical terms.

km	miles
1	0.625
1.6	1
2	1.25
3	1.875
3.2	2
4	2.5
4.8	3
5	3.125
6	3.75
6.4	4
7	4.375
8	5
9	5.625
10	6.25
16	10

you've got the space to carry it. For hot weather don't forget your sun cream and shades.

You don't have to wear specialist cycle clothing to enjoy cycling. Padded shorts, gloves, cycling shoes, cycle helmets and much more can be purchased at cycle shops if you are interested. NB It is not compulsory to wear a helmet, and the choice is yours. The CTC can provide further information on helmets if needed.

- Check your riding position is comfortable. Saddle height: when seated, place your heel on the pedal when it is at it's lowest point. Your leg should be straight, and your knee just off the locked position. On the subject of riding comfort, many bikes are supplied with saddles designed for men (long and narrow). Women may prefer to sit on a saddle designed for women (shorter and wider at the back). These are available from bike shops.

- There is some useful and information for cyclists in the *Highway Code*. This is available from garages, bookshops, and may be found in your library.

- If you think you may be cycling when it is dark, you will need to fit front and rear lights. (This is a legal requirement.) Lights and reflectors/reflective clothing are also useful in bad weather conditions.

- In the event of an accident, it is advisable to note the time and place of the incident, the names and addresses of those involved, details of their insurance company, and vehicle registration numbers and details of any witnesses. In the event of injury or damage, report the incident to the police immediately.

For further information about cycling . . .

The CTC (Cyclist's Touring Club) is Britain's largest cycling organisation, and can provide a wealth of information and advice about all aspects of cycling. The CTC works on behalf of all cyclists to promote cycling and protect cyclist's interests.

Membership includes free third-party insurance, legal aid, touring and technical information, a bi-monthly magazine and a cyclist's handbook.

For further details contact the CTC at: Cotterell House, 69 Meadrow, Godalming, Surrey GU7 3HS, or telephone 01483 417217, fax 01483 426994.

INTRODUCTION

25 Cycle Routes around Stirling and the Trossachs covers an area throughout the counties of Stirling, Clackmannan, and Falkirk on both sides of the Highland Line. From the central belt of Scotland with its unique blend of industrial heritage, ancient history, gently rolling hills and dales, to the wilder and breathtakingly beautiful Central Highlands of Scotland with its lochs, mountains, rivers, waterfalls and forests, the routes featured here leave you to choose what to sample first.

These routes vary in length from 11 kilometres to 62 kilometres and in difficulty from easy to very demanding. For the most part they use the network of minor roads with negligible traffic, which are so abundant in this part of the world and therefore ideal for cycling. Many of the routes also exploit lengths of existing cycle routes or the tow paths along Forth and Clyde and Union Canals. There are no particularly difficult surfaces to negotiate although some off-road stretches can be muddy in wet weather and sometimes the paths can be narrow.

The off-road sections featured have been checked out as well as possible to ascertain the right of way, however, sometimes it is not clear if a stretch of path is or is not a right of way, as many in Scotland are informal. In such cases the responsibility lies with the cyclist. Remember there is a law of trespass in Scotland, and although one cannot be prosecuted for crossing private land, one can be sued for damage and be asked to leave. Observe the following guidelines:

1   If you come across a sign prohibiting you from a stretch of land respect this and find an alternative route.

2   If you know the land is private try, if feasible, to get the owner's permission before riding across it.

3   If, when you are cycling on a path or stretch of land you are challenged, unless you are completely sure the land you are cycling on is public or is a right of way, then leave this land by the shortest available route.

4. When you are on any land whether private or public do not cause a nuisance in any way. Do not cause damage to crops, property, or fences.

    Close all gates and do not frighten farm animals.

5. Keep all dogs under control at all times.

If these common sense rules are applied then no one can have any justifiable grievance with you.

On occasion some of the routes use A and B class roads but I have avoided very busy roads except when they are a necessary short link with much quieter stretches of road. I feel if these roads are used properly and with care they should not cause problems and should not detract from the enjoyment of the overall route. But it's up to you to use your own judgement about safety, depending on the circumstances and your ability. If in doubt do not attempt it!

Where possible the routes start and finish at railway stations or a convenient car park. Access and refreshments (including picnics) are mentioned route-by-route. Where appropriate guidelines are given for the suitability of the ride for children.

I hope you will enjoy these routes which I feel show the area around Central Scotland at its best.

Erl B Wilkie

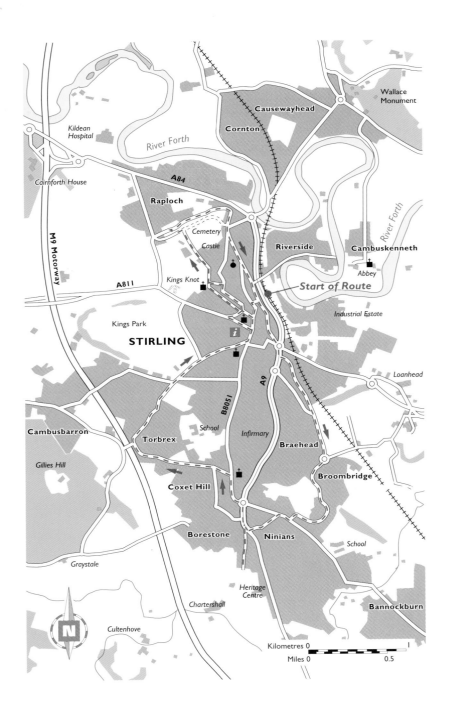

STIRLING TOWN TRAIL

Leave the car park at Stirling Station and turn left along Goosecroft Road for about 500 m, taking care along this stretch of busy road, to the Craigs roundabout. Take the fourth exit which is Burghmuir Road. Pass the entrance to Nelson Place and then dismount and turn left into Colquhoun Street, which is blocked to traffic. If however, you do not wish to negotiate this busy roundabout there is a subway beneath it, but of course, you have to walk!

Remount and follow this road, which joins with Broom Road to the roundabout a kilometre further on. Take the second exit (which is also Broom Road) and follow it for another kilometre, climbing up a slight incline to where the T-junction with Bannockburn Road is reached.

INFORMATION

Distance: 10.5 km (6.5 miles) circular route.

Map: OS Landranger, sheet 57.

Start and finish: Stirling Railway Station car park.

Terrain: Mainly flat with a short stretch of steep hill from the town centre up to the castle. The first 500 m of this route is on a busy main road and there are several busy junctions to negotiate throughout.

Refreshments: Many places to suit all tastes and pockets.

Bicycle racks in Stirling.

A pageant in Stirling.

Here turn right along Bannockburn Road for about 150m to the junction with Hill Street and turn left. Follow this road to the junction with Maitland Crescent and then turn right. Follow this road to the junction with Glasgow Road. Here turn right and take the first road on the left which is Borestone Place at the end of which the Bannock-burn Memorial and National Trust for Scotland Heritage Centre can be found.

The Heritage Centre, has an excellent exhibition of Scotland's struggle for independence and its achievement at the Battle of Bannockburn. This is followed by a chronological description of the centuries as an independent state up to the Union of the Parliaments in 1707. There is also an audio-visual theatre where a film is run every 15 minutes to explain the battle.

The Heritage Centre is close to the site of Scotland's most famous battle: Bannockburn where the Scots under the leadership of their King Robert I (the Bruce) guaranteed their independence from the English oppressors by gaining a decisive victory against a much larger force. There is also a monument to the battle in the form of a rotunda and a statue of King Robert mounted on a horse, looking east towards the site of the battle, where he had made his camp on the eve of the battle on 23 and 24 June 1314.

The route continues by returning down Borestone Place to Glasgow Road, at which point turn left and continue to the roundabout. Take the first exit which is Borestone Crescent, but changes its name several times. Continue down this road back to town.

Kirk Wynd is on the right just after the roundabout. At the end of this is the church of St Ninians of Eccles, one of the most important churches in Mediaeval Scotland. This ancient church has seen many troubled times in its history. It was successfully defended by Thomas Randolf, Earl of Moray on the eve of the Battle of Bannockburn against the marauding English army. Oliver Cromwell's troops used the church as a stable and in 1746, the church was finally destroyed by Bonnie Prince Charlie's Jacobean army, who after using the church as a store for gun powder, deliberately blew it up. All that was left was the tower which can still be seen today.

After passing Kirk Wynd take the first road on the left which is Weaver Row. After a short distance this road becomes Torbrex Road before swinging around to become Polmaise Road and ending in a roundabout. Take the second exit which is Kings Park Road bounded by fine Victorian Villas on the one side and Kings Park on the other. On reaching the end of this road turn left into Port Street, now within the bounds of Stirling town centre. At the next junction, Port Street continues as a pedestrian precinct. Here turn left into Dumbarton Road and then quickly right into Back Walk, opposite the Stirling Tourist Information Centre. Here the route passes remnants of the old town wall. This wall was strengthened in 1547 by the burgers of Stirling during the infancy of Mary Queen of Scots as a protection against attack by the army of Henry VIII during the Rough Wooing. Carry on up this short street to where it joins Corn Exchange Road. Here the municipal building is located with its interesting facade of stone carvings depicting Mary Queen of Scots and Sir William Wallace.

At this point it should be noted that you are now in the historic centre of Stirling, where, if you prefer you can park your bicycle and make your way around the many and interesting historical sites on foot. Cycle parking is provided in Back Walk and at several other sites around the town centre notably in the pedestrian precinct in Port Street. I bring this to your attention here because there is no cycle parking at Stirling Castle.

As you ride left from Corn Exchange Road and commence up Spittal Street the places of interest are numerous and could give a welcome rest from this steep hill leading towards the castle. Just a few of the places worth a visit are: The Old Town Coffee House, The Old Infirmary, The Old High School (now a hotel) and Spittal's House. Erskine Church, which now accommodates the Stirling Youth Hostel, is located a little further on up the hill where the street's name has now become St Johns Street. Next to that is Stirling Old Town Jail built in 1847 and now housing a complete audiovisual account of nineteenth century prison life.

On now a little farther to Castle Wynd, where the Collegiate Church of Holy Rude stands. This is where the infant King James VI was crowned according to Protestant rites in the presence of John Knox. Past also Mar's Wark built as a Renaissance Palace by John Erskine the Earl of Mar who served briefly as the Regent of Scotland during the reign of the infant King James VI. Finally before reaching Stirling Castle is a building known as Argyll's Lodging built by the First Earl of Stirling in 1630.

Stirling Castle was the most strategic castle in Scotland standing on a high rock which dominated the main access between the lowlands and the highlands of Scotland. It has existed in many forms since the reign of Alexander I (1107–1124). The early castle was a wooden structure which was constantly changing hands between Scots and English during the wars of independence. Therefore, after the battle of Bannockburn Robert the Bruce had the castle razed to the ground to prevent it being used by his enemies. The castle today consists of an amalgam of buildings, mostly built in the reigns of James IV, V and VI, although the outer fortifications are of a later period. The castle is approached along a lengthy esplanade which today is normally filled with cars and buses. At various places, both along the length of the esplanade and on the castle battlements, excellent views of the surrounding countryside can be enjoyed. A castle of this importance is steeped in both history and intrigue and not to make a comprehensive visit to it, would be a mistake.

On the way back down to the town centre, first to be found is the Castle Visitor Centre in Mar Place. Once back on Castle Wynd the ways back to the station are many and so I offer the following two. First via Broad Street and Baker Street leading on to King Street, and

A view of Stirling from the air.

continuing the historical tour of the old town. The the cobbles make an interesting descent before swinging left into Murray Place. At the end of this turn right at the mini roundabout into Station Road where the station can be seen.

Alternatively, turn left into Upper Castlehill and continue down to Ballengeich Road and right at Back O' Hill Road . Past Mote Hill to Lower Bridge to return to the station via Cowane Street and Goosecroft Road.

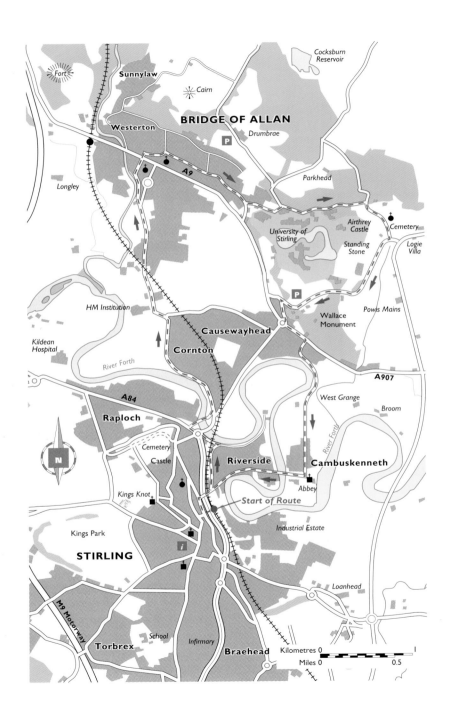

Cocksburn
Reservoir

Fort

Sunnylaw

Cairn

BRIDGE OF ALLAN

Westerton

Drumbrae

Longley

A9

Parkhead

Airthrey
Castle

Cemetery

University of
Stirling

Standing
Stone

Logie
Villa

HM Institution

Wallace
Monument

Powis Mains

Kildean
Hospital

Causewayhead

Cornton

River Forth

A907

A84

West Grange

Broom

Raploch

Cemetery

River Forth

Castle

Riverside

Cambuskenneth

Kings Knot

Abbey

Start of Route

Kings Park

Industrial Estate

STIRLING

Loanhead

N

School

Infirmary

Kilometres 0   1

Torbrex

Braehead

Miles 0   0.5

M9 Motorway

STIRLING TO BRIDGE OF ALLAN AND CAMBUSKENNETH

Leave Stirling Station car park and turn right on to Goosecroft Road. Then take the first road on the right which is Seaforth Place, and take the next left which is Forth Street. At the end of Forth Street turn left into Lovers Walk. After passing under the railway via a short tunnel and on up a slight rise, a cycle route starts taking you under the busy Customs Roundabout on the A9 and connecting with a path leading across the ancient Stirling Bridge into Bridgehaugh Road.

This stone bridge built around 1400 is not the first to have held the name Stirling Bridge. The original was of timber construction and sited a little farther downstream. It was at this bridge that Sir William Wallace won his famous victory against the English in 1297. Acts of brutality were not all confined to the English side for one of their leaders Sir Hugh Cressingham was cut down by the Scots at the battle and flayed. His skin was displayed around the country.

Turn left on to Cornton Road and carry along this for three kilometres to Bridge of Allan. (Stirling Council are currently planning a designated cycle route to Bridge of Allan.)

A bridge over the Allan Water has existed for many hundreds of years. However, up to the early part of the nineteenth century the hamlet of Bridge of Allan consisted of little more than an Inn and a few thatched cottages scattered around. Then in the 1820s mineral springs were discovered and the village became a spa for the taking of the waters. By the 1870s the waters of Bridge of Allan were so popular that 40,000 visitors a year came to partake of their mineral properties. The village grew quickly into that which can be seen today.

INFORMATION

Distance: 11–12 km (7.25 miles) circular route.

Map: OS Landranger, sheet 57.

Start and finish: Stirling Railway Station car park.

Terrain:: Mainly flat route with short undulating stretches throughout. The first few metres are on a busy main road.

Refreshments: Many places throughout the route.

Scenic view from the route.

A well laid out cycle route.

Having entered Bridge of Allan and Haws Park has been passed on the left, a Y junction is reached. Here take the left fork which is Allanvale Road. Carry along this road to Union Street which is the first turning on the right and in turn carry along this street to its end at the junction with Henderson Street. Here cross this often busy road turning into Alexander Drive and commence uphill, which is quite steep at first, to the first turning on the right – Well Road. Then turn right again into Kenilworth Road. Carry on past a four-way junction and continue past two more junctions on the left, turning left at the third which is Sheriffmuir Road. This road starts quite steeply for a short distance before levelling off. After 300 m and after passing a road going off to the left, turn right into an unmade track which is Back o' Dykes Road. Carry on around a gate and continue along this road; its wall on the right borders the grounds of Airthrey Castle which forms part of the University of Stirling.

The castle itself is now the administration block of the University. This road is not unduly rough although it can get quite muddy in prolonged spells of wet weather. However, I feel it is passable by most bicycles. At the end of this road turn right past the ruins of Old Logie Kirk and on past the present church to hold that name. At the end of this road turn right on to Hillfoots Road. Carry along this for 2 km past the imposing Wallace Monument which is situated high on top of Abbey Craig.

Wallace Monument was built in dedication to Sir William Wallace, between 1861 and 1869 and financed by the nationalist organisation the Scottish Rights Society. This massive 66 metre high stone tower, built in the Scottish baronial style and topped by an open lantern, which is a copy of the spire of St Giles Cathedral in Edinburgh. The tower can be seen from all directions over a distance of 32 km. On the ground floor there is a statue of the Scottish hero clad in chain mail, and on the second floor there is the Claymore (two handed sword) alleged to have been taken from him on his capture by the English.

After passing Wallace's Monument continue along Hillfoots Road to where it turns around a double bend at which point it becomes Logie Road and winds down hill to the junction with Alloa Road. At this junction there is a roundabout, here turn left on to the busy Alloa Road. Carry along this road for a short distance to where there is a road off to the right signposted for Cambuskenneth. Take this road known as Ladysneuk Road to its end passing the ancient village of Cambuskenneth on the way.

At the end of the road is situated the ruins of Cambuskenneth Abbey another very important historical site in this area. Cambuskenneth Abbey was founded in 1147 by King David I for the Austinian Canons. The abbey is almost all in ruins; only the completely detached campanile (bell tower) is still standing.

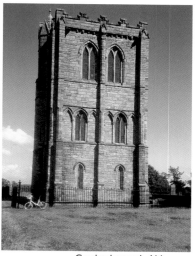

Cambuskenneth Abbey.

King James III and his Danish Queen Margaret were buried beneath the high alter of the church. In 1864 the royal couple's remains were uncovered and later they were reinterred by order of Queen Victoria.

After looking around Cambuskenneth Abbey head back into the village and turn left into South Street, at the end of which is a footbridge spanning the river Forth. Dismount and cross this bridge on foot.

Once on the other side of the river turn left, then within a few metres turn right into Abbey Road and carry along as the road changes name first to Shore Road and then Seaforth Place before it ends at Goosecroft Road. Turn left here and within a short distance Stirling Railway Station is once again reached.

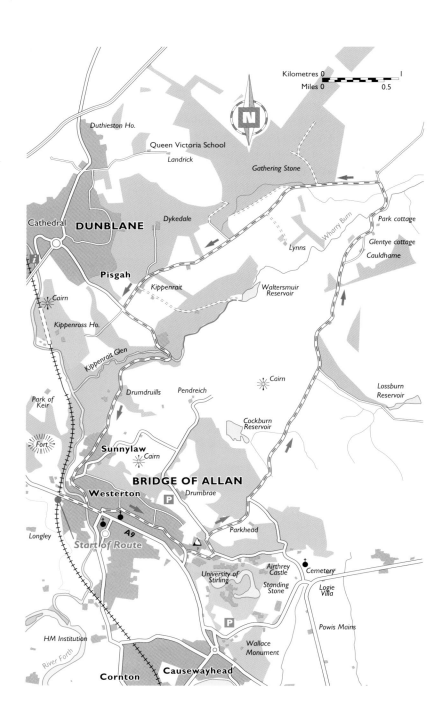

Kilometres 0   1
Miles 0   0.5

Duthieston Ho.

Queen Victoria School

Landrick

Gathering Stone

DUNBLANE

Dykedale

Cathedral

Lynns

Wharry Burn

Park cottage

Glentye cottage

Cauldhame

Pisgah

Cairn

Kippenrait

Waltersmuir Reservoir

Kippenross Ho.

Kippenrait Glen

Cairn

Lossburn Reservoir

Park of Keir

Drumdruills

Pendreich

Fort

Cockburn Reservoir

Sunnylaw

Cairn

BRIDGE OF ALLAN

Westerton

Drumbrae

Longley

A9

Parkhead

Start of Route

University of Stirling

Airthrey Castle

Cemetery

Standing Stone

Logie Villa

HM Institution

Powis Mains

River Forth

Wallace Monument

Cornton

Causewayhead

BRIDGE OF ALLAN TO SHERIFFMUIR

Leave the station car park and turn right into Station Road. Then turn left into Inverallan Road, at this point passing an old mill which has now become the offices of a firm of Chartered Surveyors. Soon the main road through Bridge of Allan is reached which is called Henderson Street. Here turn right and follow it for a little way into the village passing over the bridge spanning the Allan Water. As with the Route 2 turn into Alexander Drive, this time by turning left from Henderson Street. Commence uphill which is quite steep at first to the first turning on the right; this is Well Road which also has a fairly steep incline. Then turn right again into Kenilworth Road. Carry along this road passing a four-way junction and continuing past two more junctions on the left, and then turning left at the third into Sheriffmuir Road. Carry on up Sheriffmuir Road past the place where a right turn was made in Route 2. It is at this point the first seriously steep incline begins.

The road now begins to ascend with varying inclines, up to 1 in 5, for 1000 m. Within this stretch there is a road junction. Here take the right

INFORMATION

Distance: 19 km (11.8 miles) circular route.

Map: OS Landranger, sheet 57.

Start and Finish: Bridge of Allan Railway Station car park, where there is a rack of cycle parking stands with space for eight bicycles.

Terrain: Mainly undulating with some stretches of very steep hills throughout.

Refreshments: Many places in Bridge of Allan and also the Sheriffmuir Inn.

Bridge of Allan.

fork which is still signposted for Sheriffmuir. After this kilometre is finished, at the entrance to the Stirling Archery club, which incidentally is the steepest stretch to be found within the route, take a well earned break by admiring the fine view over the River Forth. (I recommend that you are not to be put off this route by the fact that there is such a steep incline to be negotiated for as it is only one kilometre long it can be walked in about 10 minutes, leaving you fresh to enjoy the rest of this picturesque cycle run.)

Picturesque view towards the Ochil Hills.

Carry along this picturesque undulating road as it snakes ever deeper between Sheriffmuir and the Ochil Hills for just over 5 km. At this point take the road off to the left which is signposted to Dunblane. However, before doing this linger awhile perhaps at the Sheriffmuir Inn, which is only a few metres away on the continuation of the road you are about to leave. For this point is only a few hundred metres away from the site of the Battle of Sheriffmuir. One of the earliest conflicts in the struggle to re-establish the Stuarts on the throne of the newly United Kingdom. The Union of the parliaments was by this time only a little over seven years old but many Scots were already wondering what they had done. The rising was known as the 'Fifteen' when the Earl of Mar took up arms against the forces of the first Hanovarian monarch George I. His troops were formed from the strongly Episcopalian North East and the anti Campbell clans from the west and central highlands. The, much smaller, government forces led by the Duke of Argyll met their opposition at Sheriffmuir on the 13 November 1715. The battle which ensued ended officially in stalemate. However, Argyll held the territory whilst Mar's undisciplined troops, one of whom was the notorious Rob Roy McGregor, began to melt away.

Once back to the route continue down the road towards Dunblane. After a short distance there is cairn by the road side. This cairn commemorates the men from the Clan MacRae who fell at the battle of Sheriffmuir. It was erected in 1915 by the clan.

Continue along this road from which can be seen a change in the terrain from wild moor land to a much more gentle rolling and cultivated farmland. The road continues in the usual undulating manner, passing en route Waltersmuir Reservoir, until it comes to a three-way junction, which is the 13 km point. Here take the road to the left which is signposted for Bridge of Allan. At this junction there is a sign stating that this road is closed except for cycling – that is very thoughtful of the roads authority.

After 700 m or so the road closes to traffic formally by a set of bollards installed across it. The road is now shared by cyclists and walkers only, so heed your speed on this mainly downhill stretch back to Bridge of Allan. After crossing the bridge over Wharry Burn, which further down stream flows into the Allan Water, the road continues through the woods bordering Kippenrait Glen. It then turns in land to again border the Allan Water and enters the top of the village.

Road winds through Sheriffmuir.

As the outskirts of Bridge of Allan is entered you pass the road closed sign for traffic heading in the opposite direction. Therefore from this point you will come into contact with motor vehicles once again, so take care. The road is now known as Glen Road. Continue down hill taking the right fork past, first Upper Glen Road, and Coxburn Brae. Keep right at the next junction, the beginning of Blairforkie Drive, and carry on down this hill to the junction with Henderson Road. Here turn right once again over the bridge spanning the Allan Water, then turn quickly left into Inverallan Road. From here you can retrace the route back to the station from where it began.

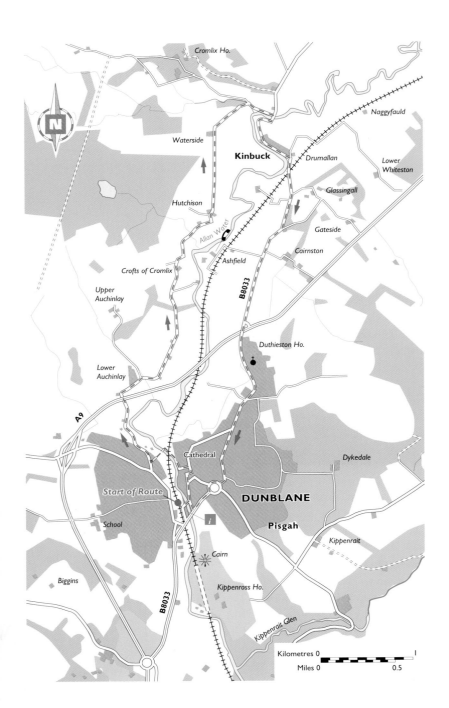

DUNBLANE TO KINBUCK

Although Dunblane is no larger than a small town it is one Scotland's most beautiful cities whose medieval Cathedral dates back to the eleventh century. It is believed that there has been a church near this spot since it was founded by seventh century missionary St Blane. The present cathedral was built by order of Bishop Clement between the years of 1233 and 1256 on the site of an earlier church. The tower of

INFORMATION

Distance: 11 km (6.87 miles) circular route.

Map: OS Landranger, sheet 57.

Start and finish: Dunblane Railway Station car park, where there is a rack of cycle parking stands with space for eight bicycles.

Terrain: Mainly undulating with no particularly strenuous hills.

Refreshments: Many places in Dunblane.

Dunblane Cathedral.

this earlier building was incorporated into the later church. By the end of the sixteenth century, due to the reformation, the cathedral was in such a state of disrepair that the roof of the nave collapsed and it remained this way until restored much later. In fact it was extensively restored on two occasions in the nineteenth century. At the cathedral there is one of the finest surviving examples of medieval wood carvings known as the 'Ochiltree Stalls'.

Dunblane is situated in a unique location almost equidistant from Glasgow, Edinburgh and Dundee, with Stirling and Perth considerably closer still. It has direct connections by both road and rail to all these locations, and has therefore become a most desirable residential location. Dunblane is built on both sides of the Allan Water which meanders through the town centre. It also supports the oldest library in Scotland, namely Leighton library

Look over the Allan Water to the Cathedral.

established by Robert Leighton Bishop of Dunblane in 1687.

Leave the railway station by way of Stirling Road until High Street is reached. This has to be done on foot, because it is a one way street in the opposite direction. Once in High Street mount and go on to The Cross, where Dunblane Cathedral, Leighton Library and Cathedral Museum are located. Ride around three sides of the Cathedral yard into Haining. Carry on this road as it makes a 90 degree turn at the edge of a steep bank down to the Allan Water. This road then runs under the railway soon after which it ends. To continue over Fairy Bridge, which is for pedestrians, you have to dismount. But you can remount at the other side of the bridge where the path connects with the junction of Kilbryde Crescent and Auchinlay Road. Here turn right into Auchinlay Road and follow this minor road out of Dunblane. Continue to follow this road as it follows the route of the river. Soon there is a 90 degree bend in the road from which vantage point a good view back towards Dunblane can be enjoyed. The road then commences under the busy A9. After the bridge there then follows the steepest climb to be found on this route which is about 300 m long.

Looking east past the A9 as it snakes its way north–south a large building can be seen in the distance. This is Queen Victoria School for the children of Servicemen who have served in Scottish regiments. The school is a memorial to the soldiers who fell in the South African War. Amongst many other things the school has a very fine Pipe Band which for many years has played before the huge crowd awaiting their country's victory in rugby's five nations championship at Murrayfield in Edinburgh.

After 5 km a junction is reached. Here turn right and follow this road for a short distance to the T-junction with the B8033. Here once again turn right and cross the beautiful stone double arch bridge taking this road over the Allan Water. Follow the road down hill into the small village of Kinbuck where there was once situated two woollen mills but alas little industry still exists. On the south side of the village there is a short sharp hill to climb but it lasts only for a hundred metres or so.

Carry along this road, passing this time over the A9, then past the Queen Victoria School and into the northern part of Dunblane.

Midway down the road between Kinbuck and the bridge over the A9 is located a road on the right which carries on down to the almost hidden village of Ashfield. Ashfield grew up around the now closed dyeworks. If you would like to explore this small village it will add approximately one kilometre to the journey.

Peaceful street scene, Dunblane.

Soon the Stakis hotel (formally Dunblane Hydro) is located on the left side of the road. This monument to Victorian opulence was opened in 1878 as a Hydropathic establishment which specialised in many varieties of baths such as, mustard, electric, medicated etc. This coupled by fresh air and a rigid diet was thought to be, with some reason, an aid to good health.

On to the roundabout and take the second exit which is the Stirling Road (the former Perth Road, and still a dual carriageway). Follow this road down hill taking the first turning on the right, almost at St Blane's bridge over the Allan Water. This is Beech Road, and then go left over Old Bridge leading to Dunblane Station.

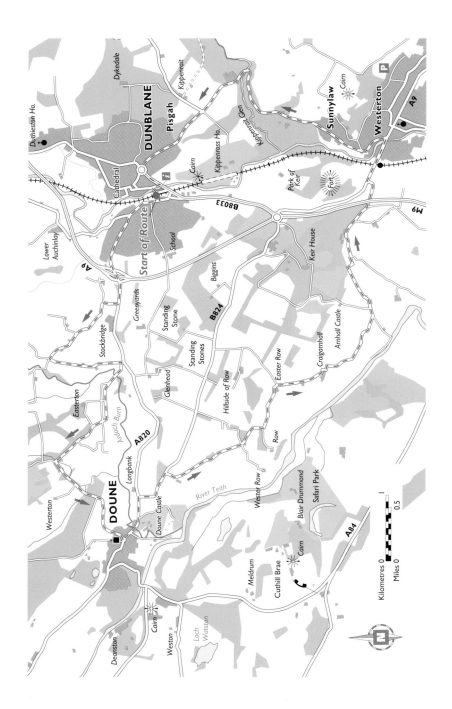

DUNBLANE TO BRIDGE OF ALLAN VIA DOUNE

Leave Dunblane Station car park and turn right on to Springfield Terrace. After a short distance this road changes its name to Doune Road (A820). Follow this road for just over a kilometre, passing over the A9 en route, to a minor road junction signposted for Stockbridge. Turn right on to this road and follow it for a kilometre to a four-way junction and turn left. In turn follow this road through pleasant farm land back towards the Doune Road. However, a few metres before reaching this main road, take the minor road on the right, signposted for Argaty. After about 2 km a T-junction is reached. Here turn left and follow the road a further 2 km into Doune. On entering Doune the road becomes King Street; at the end you should turn left into Main Street which is the A820. Continue out of the village, passing the entrance to Doune Castle on the right, to the junction with the B824 signposted to Bridge of Allan, and join this road.

INFORMATION

Distance: 24 km (15 miles) circular route.

Map: OS Landranger, sheet 57.

Start and finish: Dunblane Railway Station has a rack of cycle parking stands with space for eight bicycles. If travelling to Dunblane by train you will have to cross the footbridge first to gain access to Dunblane Station car park.

Terrain: Mainly undulating with no particularly strenuous hills.

Refreshments: Many places in Dunblane, Bridge of Allan and Doune.

A profusion of rosehips.

Once on to the B824 it is but a short distance to the minor road found at the first turning on the right. Whilst on the B824 take care, for even although it is a B category road there can be fast moving vehicles on it. Once on the minor road you will scarcely see any traffic of any sort save perhaps the occasional farm vehicle. This road is once again undulating, but there are no particularly long steep stretches to cause you any particular problems. Continue past Inverardoch Mains Farm and on to the junction at Row House and bear left. At this point the road surface deteriorates with some potholes and grass growing through the surface at various points.

The next junction to be reached is at Easter Row. Here take the road to the right where the road surface improves once again. On now past Craigarnhall Farm: here the road has an abundance of wildlife on and around it. There are rabbits by

A serene view of Dunblane.

the score, the occasional hare and plenty of game birds who all seem to be oblivious to the presence of a passing cyclist. Perhaps they won't be so indifferent towards the falcon circling patiently overhead. There is a good view of Wallace's Monument and the surrounding countryside to be had from this point. There is now a fairly steep hill to descend. There are however, a few very tight bends on this stretch and in places the road surface is less than good. So be careful to keep to a speed which takes account of these problems. The road soon passes a terrace of what looks to be estate houses after that it broadens out as it turns under the M9 motorway.

After the underpass the road climbs up to the A9, 100 m further on. Turn right at this junction and follow the road down to the bridge over the Allan Water, at the beginning of Bridge of Allan. After crossing the bridge turn left into Blairforkie Drive and travel up this road retracing, in the opposite direction, the route described at the end of Route 3. From the end of Blairforkie Drive veer left into Glen Road. Continue past the road closed sign, which is meant for motorised vehicles and on to the wooded track meandering past Kippenrait Glen. After being on this road for about 3 km a junction is reached where the road to the right goes off to Sheriffmuir. Here carry straight on to Dunblane 1.5 km farther on. At the end of this road which is still known as Glen Road a roundabout is reached. Here take the first exit onto the Stirling Road (the former Perth Road and still a dual carriageway). Follow this road down hill taking the first turning on the right, almost at St Blane's bridge over the Allan Water, into Beach Road. Then turn left over Old Bridge leading to Dunblane Station.

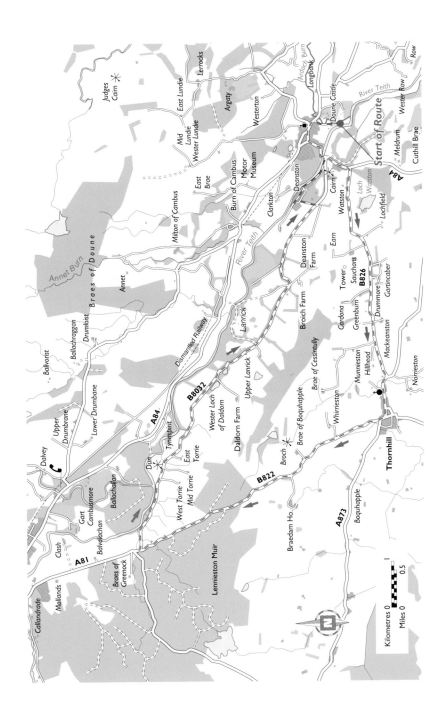

DOUNE TO THORNHILL VIA DEANSTON

The car park of Doune Castle is one of only two official car parks in the vicinity of the village, the other being at Castlehill. Whilst in Doune most visitors, I'm sure, will take the opportunity to visit this fine Castle situated between the river Teith and the Ardoch Burn. It is a fine example of an internal courtyard castle. It was used as a residence but it was a good stronghold, with its defences centred around the gatehouse keep. The castle was built by Robert Stewart, the first Duke of Albany, brother of King Robert III, who became Regent of Scotland during the imprisonment, in England, of James I.

After the death of Robert, the castle was inherited by his son Murdoch the second Earl of Albany. On the return of James I to Scotland, Murdoch was beheaded along with his son Alexander and his Father-in-law the Earl of Lennox, for the crime of 'Roboria' which translated means unconstitutional violence. King James then confiscated the lands and the castle from the house of Albany. Over the next few hundred years the castle was used as a royal residence, a state prison and a dower house for the widowed Queens of Scotland. Mary Queen of Scots lived in the castle from time to time where she had a suite of rooms over the kitchens. During the turbulent times of the sixteenth century the castle was besieged and was the place where plots and counter plots were hatched and revenged. Since this time the castle has been the property of the Earls of Moray.

The castle was occupied by the Duke of Montrose in 1645, but suffered little during the Civil War. One hundred years later the castle was seized by the

INFORMATION

Distance: 25 km (15.6 miles) circular route.

Map: OS Landranger, sheet 57.

Start and finish: Doune Castle car park.

Terrain: Mainly undulating route with no particularly strenuous hills. The short stretch along the A84 can often be busy.

Refreshments: Many places in Doune, Deanston and Thornhill.

Doune Castle.

Jacobites and used as a prison. By the end of the eighteenth century the castle lay unoccupied and unroofed. It was extensively restored around 1883, by order of the 14th Earl of Moray with the restoration team being led by Andrew Kerr an Edinburgh architect. Lately, the castle has undergone more extensive restoration by Historic Scotland.

At the end of the castle driveway at the junction of Main Street turn left and head into the centre of the village of Doune to where the ancient Mercat Cross is located. Here turn left and commence down George Street, a one way street, to its end at Stirling Road (A84) where Muir Hall is found. Turn left on to this generally busy road, heading downhill and out of the village. Cross the Bridge of Teith which was built in 1535, and although widened in 1866, it was obviously built to carry more serene forms of transportation than today's traffic. Continue along this road for almost a kilometre to the junction with the B826. Here take this road and follow its undulating route, generally uphill, for 4.5 km to the junction with the A873. Turn right here following this road through Thornhill.

Thornhill is a small mainly agricultural village almost all of it being located on the Main Street. At the Western end of the village, turn right on to the B822. In turn follow this road, generally downhill, but with the occasional short steep gradient uphill, to the junction with B8032 and turn left. This road mostly follows the route of the beautiful river Teith as it meanders back towards Doune. Once at the junction with the B8032 however, if you wish to deviate from the route it is only about 2 km into Callander along the A81 which is found a few metres further along the B822.

A well developed set of rams horns.

The first stretch of the B8032 is through woodland with the river running close by with pleasant views along its banks. This river is, not surprisingly, well-used by fishermen who can be seen standing in the water, casting their rod and line, in the hopes of catching a Brown Trout, Sea Trout or even, depending on the season a salmon. It was around here, so the story goes, that during the terrible frost of 1894/95, which lasted from November to April, whilst walking along the frozen River Teith a local man saw a large salmon stuck fast in the ice. He then hacked through the ice with a pickaxe and extracted the fish which he took home to his family. The river Teith rises from two lochs which are Vennachar and Lubnaig, and flows into the river Forth just to the north west of Stirling.

An old model at Thornhill fair.

Carry on along this road which in my experience is not usually busy to where a wall can be found by the roadside. This high wall, which continues for a considerable distance, is the boundary of the Lanrick Estate. After passing the estate it is only two kilometres or so to the junction signposted for Deanston. Turn left here and cycle downhill past a housing estate. At the bottom of the hill turn left into Leny Road and continue along to the junction with Teith Road and turn sharp right. In turn follow this road as it runs parallel with the mill lade of the former cotton mill which, until recently, was the largest employer in the area, outwith agriculture. Turn left at the primary school and then quickly right and follow the road running parallel with the River Teith on the left. On the other side of the road the old cotton mill buildings, now used as a distillery, can be found.

At the next junction turn left back on to the B8032. Almost immediately turn left again on to the A84 and cross the bridge of Teith once again. Continue uphill past the War Memorial and turn right into Balkerach Street, which at Mercat Cross becomes Main Street from where it is but a short distance back to the castle car park.

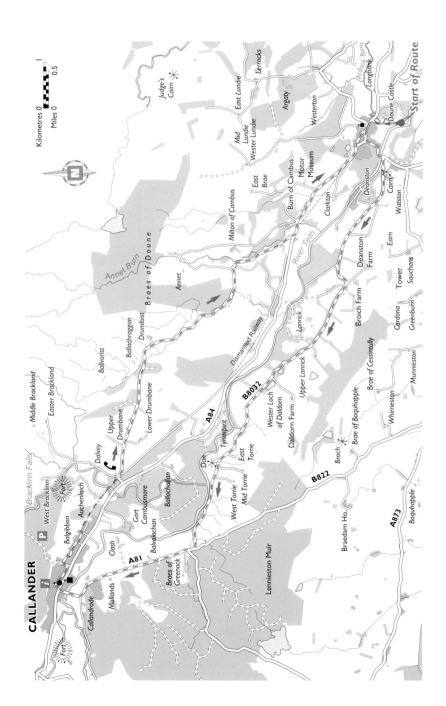

DOUNE TO CALLANDER

As with the last route this one also starts at the car park of Doune Castle. In fact the first part of this route is identical to the last. At the end of the castle driveway is the junction of Main Street turn left and head into the centre of the village of Doune. Here bear left at the Mercat Cross and commence down George Street, which is one way. Go to the end to Stirling Road. Here turn left and follow this quite busy road out of the village. Cross the Bridge of Teith and turn right immediately on to the B8032 and carry along this road for 10 km to the junction with the B822. Turn right here and after a short distance the A81 is reached. Carry straight on for 2 km into Callander.

Callander town is very popular with tourists. However there has been a settlement here since before Roman times. During Roman times it was the site of a large Roman Military Camp. There was also a Roman Fort half a kilometre further to the west. This location between the high ground to the north and the River Teith to the south has always been a main route between the Highlands and the Lowlands and therefore a place of much conflict.

St Kessog, the sixth century evangelist from Ireland, is said to have preached and performed miracles at the place where a mound stands close to

INFORMATION

Distance: 25 km (15.6 miles) circular route.

Map: OS Landranger, sheet 57.

Start and finish: Doune Castle car park.

Terrain: Mainly undulating with no particularly strenuous hills. The last 2 km along the A84 can often be very busy.

Refreshments: Many places in Doune, and Callander.

St Kessogs mound.

Top: View over the river Teith at Callander.

Bottom: Sunset on the river Teith.

the bridge across the Teith on Bridge Street. The mound, bearing the name of the saint (Tom-na-Chessaig), is thought to be a twelfth century motte and bailey, but there is little evidence to prove this theory, although its size and shape would suggest this is the case.

The town has grown since Sir Walter Scott brought the Trossachs area to prominence through his immortal poem 'The Lady of the Lake' and his story of Rob Roy, the infamous seventeenth century bandit, which brought tourists flocking into the area. Even the first tourist guide was written as early as 1780. These early tourists included, Coleridge, Keats, DeQuincey, Lamb, Wordsworth, Tennyson and Ruskin. Almost a century later the railway was opened which further asserted Callander's importance as a tourist resort. Alas this railway is now closed with the only consolation that part of it is now a cycleway.

Within the former St Kessog's church in Ancaster Square is located the tourist information centre and a permanent exhibition devoted to Rob Roy.

On entering Callander at Bridge Street, cross Main Street and on into Cross Street. At the end of this turn right into Glenartney Road and then right into North Church Street. Take the first street on the left, Craigard Road, and follow this to the junction of Bracklinn Road which takes its name from the Bracklinn Falls a little further to the north. These beautiful falls are worth a visit but only on foot from the car park at the end of Bracklinn Road which is 2km further north. It is interesting to note that Arden House is also a little further up Bracklinn Road. This is the house used in the television adaptation of AJ Cronin's Doctor Finlay's Casebook.

At Bracklinn Junction jink right then left into Murdiston Avenue, which has no access to vehicular traffic at this point, and follow it to where it joins Livingstone Avenue. In turn continue along this a few metres to the junction with Glen Gardens, where on the other side of the road a cycle route begins which is clearly signposted. This cycle route is part of the Central Highland Way which will eventually go from Stirling to Killin and Crianlarich. It also will also form part of the National Cycle Route which is currently being developed by Sustrans the National Cycling Charity. Some of this route will also form part of the Inverness to Dover route.

Follow this cycle route to its end one and a half kilometres further on. At the end of the cycle route just beyond the beautiful old stone arch, Kelty Bridge, turn left onto a minor road. Within 200 metres a road junction is reached. Be careful here for there are heavy quarry vehicles using this stretch of road coming to and from the quarry private access road. Pass this access road and immediately there is another minor road off to the right. This road is marked by a red sign with Drunbane marked upon it. This road is in fact the Drumloist Road. Carry on along this undulating road for 11 km to where it joins the A84. Here turn left, taking care when joining this main road at it is often busy, and carry on along it for almost 3 km back to Doune. After being on the A84 for one kilometre another minor road is passed. This is the access to the Doune Motor Museum with its 50 exhibits including the second oldest Rolls Royce in the world.

Once in Doune turn left into Balkerach Street, which at Mercat Cross becomes Main Street from where it is but a short distance back to Doune Castle.

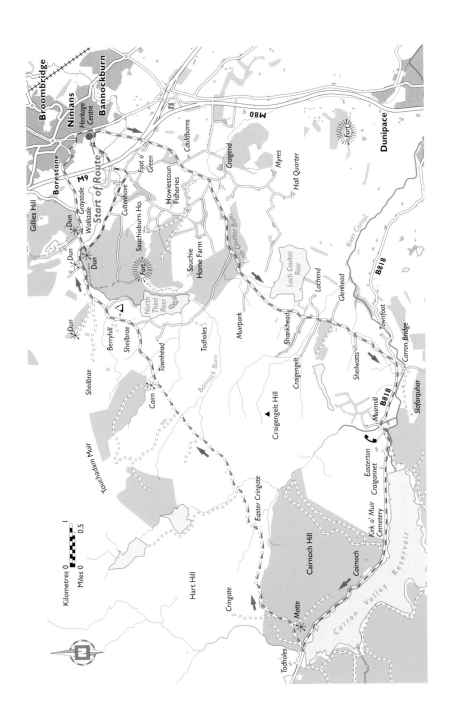

STIRLING TO CARRON BRIDGE

On leaving the car park head for the Glasgow Road and turn right. Then immediately turn right again into Fairhill Road. Following the signs for Carron Bridge make one more quick turn this time to the left into New Line Road.

Once on this minor road there follows a slight incline up to the bridge over the M9. After this continue uphill to a crossroads. Here carry straight on still following the signs for Carron Bridge. There are a couple of 90 degree bends on this route so take care. At the next junction veer to the right through rolling pasture land for 2 km and on to another junction halfway through a wooded area. Here take the left fork, which is once again the road to Carron Bridge. The road continues to climb for a further 2 km sometimes quite steeply for short distances. Go past Loch Coultar Reservoir, to the junction with the B818 at the Carron bridge Hotel. The hotel is marked Inn on the map.

You may be interested to note that this route has now joined another route featured in *25 Cycle Routes Around Glasgow* which is another book in the series by the same author.

From here turn right on to the B818. Two and a half kilometres along the B818 is the eastern entrance to the Carron Valley Forest where the forestry roads, skirting the south side of the reservoir, can be explored.

Continue along the B818, with its very picturesque views to the south over the Campsie Fells - from Dumgoyne in the west to Meikle Bin and beyond in the east. The route takes you almost to the western extremity of the Carron Valley Reservoir where a road junction is reached. This road is very minor and the junction is not clearly defined. There is a sign marking a new development by East of Scotland Water which will help you to identify the junction.

INFORMATION

Distance: 32 km (20 miles) circular route.

Map: OS Landranger, sheet 57.

Start and finish: The National Trust (for Scotland) Heritage Centre car park. Or alternatively this route could begin and end at Stirling Railway Station. If you prefer the latter then start and finish with the route described from the station to the Heritage Centre in Route 1. This will add 8 km to the total journey.

Terrain: Long distance with some very long steep hills. The worst is the minor road past Earl's Hill which ascends 120 m in 5 miles with short stretches of up to 1 in 10 gradients. This route is not recommended for children.

Refreshments: Many places in Stirling and the Carron Bridge Hotel.

Bridge over the Bannock burn.

If the cyclist stays on the B818 for another kilometre the Loup of Fintry is reached, where the Endrick cascades down 30 m from the high moorland into the valley below. This beautiful waterfall is worth the short detour to visit.

Once on this minor road the climbing commences and does so at varying degrees of steepness up to 1 in 10 for almost 6 km, although the steep stretches are all short.

After half a kilometre there is a forestry road off to the right where my second detour begins. You could take this turning and ride up the hill for half a kilometre to the car park. On an open area next to this car park is the location of the Motte which belonged to John de Graham of Dundaff, who was a friend of Sir William Wallace. Graham joined Wallace in the early days of the struggle for Scottish independence and was considered to be, next to Wallace himself, the most valiant of the Scots. John de Graham was killed at the battle of Falkirk and his body is buried in the old churchyard in Falkirk Parish Church; now the site of a monument erected to this brave warrior. It was said by Blind Harry, the chronicler of Wallace's life, that Wallace was found weeping over the body of his friend de Graham when he was discovered lying on the battlefield after the battle.

The Motte was built by Sir David de Graham the founder of the house of Montrose, who was probably the grandfather of John, in 1237. The sword used by de Graham is still held by his descendent the Duke of Montrose.

From this Motte there is a beautiful view over the Carron Valley Reservoir and the hills beyond.

Return to the minor road once again and continue the ascent passing through areas of woodland, some deciduous and some evergreen, to where the moorland starts. Here the road passes first Hart Hill and then Earl's Hill with its television transmitter on top. There are four cattle grids on this stretch of road so take care when negotiating them.

At the top of the hill there is a wonderful view over the Forth valley where on a clear day one can see the Forth Bridges and Edinburgh beyond.

The road now begins its long descent which makes for exhilarating cycling. However once again a word of warning: there are a few nasty bends on the way down this road so watch your speed. Remember also, cars do use this road and although you may have seen very few so far, you could come upon one at any time. So take care!

A road junction is soon reached. Here carry straight on past the North Third Reservoir with its back drop of dramatic rocky crags keeping on this road for two and a half kilometres passing two road junctions. The road passes an MOD firing range where on occasion it may be possible to see, from the safety of the road, some tanks on manoeuvres. The road then continues on through a wooded glade following the route of the Bannock Burn past the first road junction.

Once again and for the last time the road climbs to where it broadens out at the second junction. This broader road soon turns at right angles to a much smaller minor one. Here take the minor road down hill and across the bridge over the M9 motorway. After crossing the motorway, the road turns at right angles and enters a housing estate at which point it is called Gateside Road. Carry on past three roads on the left: Howlands Road, Bearside Road and Barnsdale Road. Continue into Newpark Crescent then turn right at the end into Newpark Road, then right into Nailer Road. Finally turn into Borestone Place at the end of which Bannockburn Memorial is situated. From this point, dismount and walk to the car park or return to town using one of the routes described in Route 1.

View over the Forth Valley.

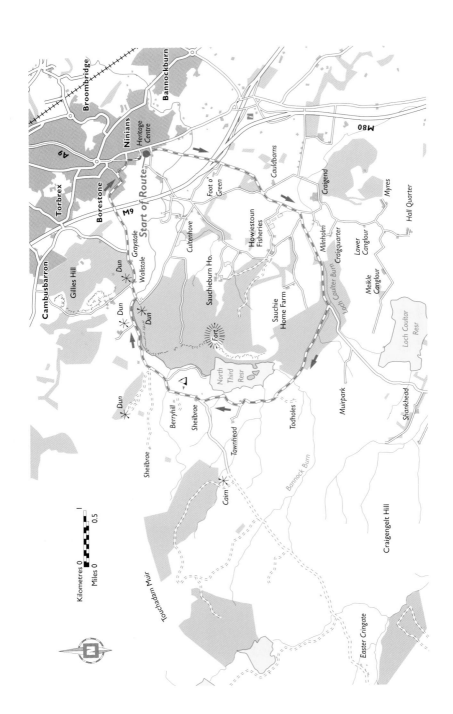

Kilometres 0
0.5
1
Miles 0

STIRLING TO NORTH THIRD RESERVOIR

As with the last route, on leaving the car park head for the Glasgow Road then turn right. Immediately turn right again into Fairhill Road. Following the signs for Carron Bridge, make one more quick turn this time to the left into New Line Road. Once on this minor road there follows a slight incline up to the bridge over the M9. After this continue uphill to a cross-roads. Here carry straight on still following the signs for Carron Bridge. There are a couple of 90 degree bends on this route so take care. At the next junction veer to the right through rolling pasture land for another 2 km and on through a wooded area to where another junction is reached.

Here take the right fork and commence along a 3 m wide minor road, with woods on both sides for a kilometre or so, before open country is once again located: first on one side of the road and then on both. En route along this road there is the North Third Reservoir which is a very popular location for fishing and other water sports. On its eastern side there stands a long outcrop of rock known as the Sauchie Craig which is the edge of a Dolomite plug extending for 3 km to the north. The reason that it is exposed is because the adjacent softer sandstone has eroded away over millions of years leaving these high and dramatic rocky crags open to the elements. This is an excellent environment for birds and there are many interesting varieties to be found.

The final stretch of this road is where the steepest stretch of incline is to be found on this route, however, it is not long. From here a road junction is soon reached at which a turn to the right will bring the reader back on to

INFORMATION

Distance: 13 km (8.12 miles) circular route.

Map: OS Landranger, sheet 57.

Start and finish: Heritage Centre car park. Or alternatively you could begin and end at Stirling Railway Station. If you prefer the latter, then follow directions from the station to the Heritage Centre in Route 1. This will add 8 km to the total journey.

Terrain: Uphill in varying degrees of steepness for 3/4 of its total distance. The descent is quick and steep. Therefore, great care should be taken to control your speed. Fairly strenuous.

Refreshments: Many places in Stirling.

Old and new cycles.

A group of cyclists enjoying a chat before moving off.

the road mentioned in the last route. Descend for 2 km stretch past the MOD land and alongside the Bannock Burn.

Soon after this, the road once again and for the last time, begins to climb to where it broadens out at the second junction. This broader road soon turns at right angles and a much smaller minor road continues straight on. Here take the minor road down hill and across the bridge over the M9 motorway. After the motorway has been crossed, the road turns at right angles and enters a housing estate at which point the road is called Gateside Road. Carry on past three roads on the left: Howlands Road, Bearside Road and Barnsdale Road and continue into Newpark Crescent. At the end of it turn right into Newpark Road, then right into Nailer Road, and finally into Borestone Place. Bannockburn Memorial is situated at the end of Borestone Place. From this point, dismount and walk to the car park or commence back to town using one of the routes described in Route 1.

An alternative route back is, once having turned right at North Third Reservoir and followed this road for 2 km a small road junction is reached on the right. This junction, which could easily be missed, has a concrete bridge over the Bannock Burn. Turn right here and follow this narrow unmade track as it turns west for a short distance before turning south east.

Because this track is not surfaced, it is rough with many potholes, but it is not so bad as would prevent cycling by most types of bicycle. Continue along this track for 2 km, past two little fishing lochs at Swanswater Fishery, to the next junction. Here turn left and follow this road for a hundred metres or so to a T-junction at which point once again turn left. Follow this road over the motorway and past Chartershall to where Bruce's statue can be seen on the hill next to the road. Follow the road around to where it joins the Glasgow Road. Turn left here and within a few metres the Heritage Centre is once again reached.

The 'Old Brig' at Chartershall.

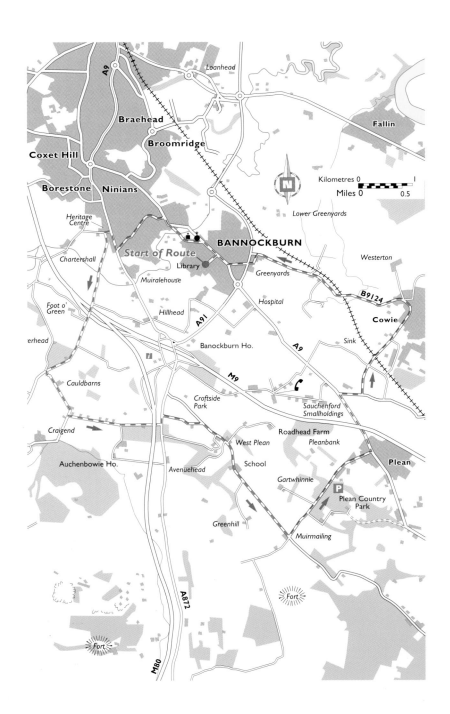

Loanhead

A9

Braehead

Broomridge

Coxet Hill

Fallin

Borestone   Ninians

Heritage
Centre

Chartershall

Kilometres 0   I
Miles 0   0.5

N

Lower Greenyards

BANNOCKBURN

Start of Route

Library

Muiralehouse

Greenyards

Westerton

Foot o'
Green

Hillhead

Hospital

B9124

Cowie

A91

erhead

Banockburn Ho.

A9

Sink

Cauldbarns

M9

Croftside
Park

Sauchenford
Smallholdings

Craigend

Roadhead Farm
Pleanbank

West Plean

Auchenbowie Ho.

Avenuehead

School

Plean

Gartwhinnie

P

Greenhill

Plean Country
Park

Muirmailing

A872

Fort

M80

Fort

BANNOCKBURN TO PLEAN COUNTRY PARK

Bannockburn is an ancient village which takes its name from the burn running through its centre. The route begins west along Quakerfield and after only a few metres turns left into Main Street and continues on to the Brae, at the bottom of which the Old Town bridge or Spittal Bridge, over the Bannock Burn is located. This is the site of a medieval fort. The bridge is alleged to have been built by order of Robert Spittal who was King James IV's tailor after he had had a serious soaking whilst trying to negotiate the burn on horse back. Continue on up hill to where the junction with New Road is reached. Dismount and cross this junction which is blocked off to traffic. Continue west along New Road to the first junction on the left which is Firs Entry; this soon becomes Morrison Drive and then Milton Road. Go to the end of the road to the junction with Milton Terrace (Glasgow Road). Here turn right and follow this road for a short distance to the junction with Fairhill Road and turn left. As with the last two Routes once again turn left into New Lane Road and follow it to the four-way junction. This time though turn left on to the minor road which heads south east.

After a little under one kilometre a road junction is reached. Turn left here following this road, pass Auchenbowie Caravan Park, going under the M9 motorway to the junction of the adjacent A872. Here turn left and follow this road for a few metres only, and then turn right into a small unmade minor road linking with the Roman Road to West Plean 300 m or so farther on. On reaching the Roman road turn right and follow it

INFORMATION

Distance: 13 (8.12 miles) km circular route.

Map: OS Landranger, sheet 57 and 65.

Start and finish: The public library car park, Quakerfield Bannockburn.

Terrain: Undulating but without steep hills; it is not difficult. The short stretches along the A9 can often be busy.

Refreshments: Places in Bannockburn, Plean and Cowie.

Old mill at Bannockburn.

for 2 km, past West Plean, to a four-way junction and turn left.

After cycling down this road for almost a kilometre the entrance to Plean Country Park can be found on the right. This park was once the estate of wealthy East India trader William Simpson who had the house built in the beginning of the 19th century in the earlier Georgian style. The estate also boasts extensive stables and a large walled garden. Unfortunately both the house and stables are currently in a dangerous condition and therefore fenced off, the former being extensively damaged by fire as recently as 1970. Another eminent owner of this property in modern times was Sir Peter Thorneycroft who served as the member of Parliament for Monmouth in Wales and who became the President of the Board of Trade in the Labour Government of 1945.

The park today, with its statue of a coal miner commemorating the industry which until recently dominated this part of the world, is a pleasant and tranquil place. Its beautiful tree lined avenues and areas of woodland are home to a large variety of wildlife including deer and woodpeckers.

Spittal bridge over the Bannock burn.

On leaving Plean Country Park turn right and follow the road into the village of Plean. Once the A9 is reached turn left and take this main road for a little less than a kilometre passing under the M9 motorway. Turn right on to the road which is signposted to Cowie, and within a short distance it joins the B9124. Follow this road to the left and within a kilometre this small ex-mining village is reached. On entering the village the road becomes Main Street, at the end turn left. Keeping to the B9124, on to the Bannockburn Road continue for 2.5 km back into Bannockburn. Once on this part of the road one can see a beautiful panoramic view from Alloa to Stirling with a backdrop of the Ochil Hills behind.

When the beginning of Bannockburn has been reached and only a matter of a few metres before the junction with the A9, turn left onto a small road which is an access road to Greenyards Nursery. Just before the entrance to this garden centre turn right and after dismounting take the gate out on to the A9 and cross this busy road with care. On the other side there is another gate leading into Stein Square: at the end turn right into Newmarket. Commence down this road which soon changes its name to Quakerfield and here on the left is the public library where the route began.

I myself have an affinity for Bannockburn for my father's family lived in the village for a time. Indeed my grandfather was fatally injured in the horrific multiple train crash at Beattock in 1914, whilst he and his regiment were on their way to the Western Front. He is buried in Bannockburn Cemetery.

Gymkhana, en route.

DENNY TO CARRON VALLEY RESERVOIR

It has been said that Denny and Dunipace are situated in the bottleneck of Scotland, for they are nestling at the extreme western end of the Falkirk Carse, in the foothills of the Campsie Fells. As with Stirling, throughout the centuries people wishing to pass the area could not do so without passing directly through this location. It was therefore the scene of many a conflict: first between the Ancient Britons, the Scots, and the Romans. Indeed as the remains of Antonine's Wall lie a very short distance to the south of Denny it is reasonable to assume this area saw much of the Romans during their short occupation of Central and Southern Scotland. Later the Scots and the English were to realise the area's strategic importance as they fought each other for the sovereignty of Scotland.

Although the parishes of Denny and Dunipace came into existence in 1601 the present villages developed during the industrial revolution. Calico printing, dying and bleaching, paper making and the mining of iron ore fed the insatiable demands of the surrounding iron foundries. Alas most of these industries are no longer in the area.

This route begins in the centre of Denny, close to the four-way junction consisting of Duke Street on the west, Broad Street on the east, Stirling Street on the north and Glasgow Road to the south. From the car park turn right into Duke Street and continue along it to the junction with Nethermains Road and turn left. Carry along this road for a short distance to the first junction on the right which is the B818 signposted for Carron Bridge.

> ### INFORMATION
>
> **Distance:** 19 km (11.87 miles) circular route.
>
> **Map:** OS Landranger, sheet 57.
>
> **Start and finish:** Car park at the back of the public library, just off Duke Street, Denny.
>
> **Terrain:** Many steep hills particularly on the first half; it is quite strenuous.
>
> **Refreshments:** Places in Denny, Topps Farm and the Carron Bridge Hotel.

Autumn colours on the route.

Turn right on to this road which winds gradually uphill for the first kilometre passing under the M80 en route past the small village of Stoneywood. Continue uphill to the next village of Fankerton.

Fankerton is one location where it is known that a battle between the marauding Picts and the Romans took place. This battle would have been as much to protect the local tribes people against the Picts as to protect the Romans themselves. The battle was at the ford of the River Carron and it was said to have been so fierce that the river ran red with blood for miles. Indeed legend has it that from that day on, the land around the area where the battle was fought was known as Red Brae.

After Fankerton the road continues uphill for the next 6 km, sometimes fairly steeply and for prolonged periods, more or less all the way to Carron Bridge. On the way up stop. You will probably have to – I certainly did many times – and take in the view over the Fintry and Campsie Hills, the obvious landmarks being Meikle Bin on the left and Earl's Hill with its television mast on the right. One passes, en route, Topps Farm Guest House and Restaurant where refreshment can be had. After this it is a short distance over the masonry arch bridge spanning the River Carron and on into Stirling Council territory to Carron Bridge with the hotel of the same name where refreshment can also be had.

Carry on for two and a half kilometres along the B818 to the eastern entrance of the Carron Valley Forest, from where it is possible to cycle around this picturesque place on forestry roads with beautiful views over the Carron Valley Reservoir and the surrounding hills.

At this point return by the same route along the B818, back into the Falkirk Council area, for 5.5 km then turn right into a minor road. Here there are two roads side by side. The first gives access to the site of a civil engineering works, so take the second turning.

It's uphill on this road, but this time the gradient is fairly gradual, passing through a farmyard en route. At the top of this kilometre long hill, a junction is reached. Turn right. Now continue on this flat road as it runs with the contours of the adjacent hills. Along this stretch of road there is an incredible view over the river Forth with Longannet Power Station on the left and Grangemouth to the right, with the Forth Bridges clearly visible behind.

Danish cyclists making the ascent into the Fintry hills.

The road soon begins to descend back down towards Denny passing Myot Hill, which is the site of an iron age fort. There are some fairly tight bends on this stretch of road so take care not to travel too fast. Soon a four-way junction is reached. Here turn left and continue to circumnavigate Myot Hill, clearly still considered of strategic significance as it has a radar station on top of it. On now past Myot Hill House which is an equestrian centre where with luck many horses may be seen galloping around the adjacent fields.

The outskirts of Denny is soon reached and after passing under the M80 once again this minor road ends at Nethermains Road. Turn left here and after passing the junction of the B818 on the left retrace the route back to the car park.

A splash of colour by the roadside.

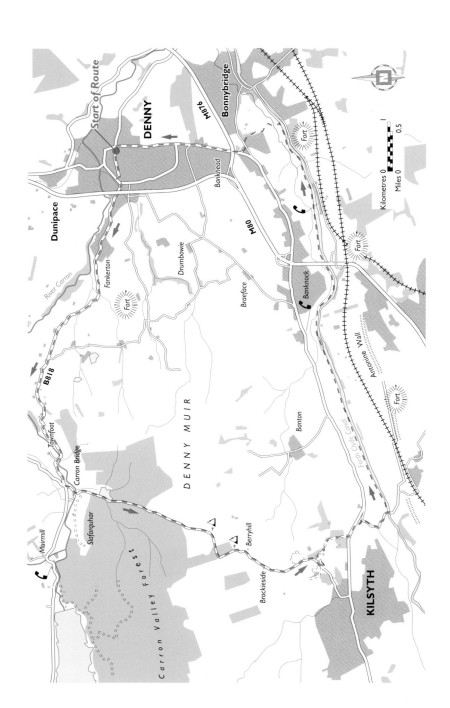

DENNY TO FORTH AND CLYDE CANAL

This route is exactly as that described in Route 11 until it reaches the Carron Bridge Hotel.

Having got to the top of this hill there will be a certain feeling of achievement and perhaps just a little excitement at the thought of the exhilarating descent to follow Indeed there could be no greater an exhilarating descent than down the Tak-ma-doon Road almost into Kilsyth. However just a little word of caution is necessary at this point: this road descends 263 m in five kilometres with short stretches of up to 1 in 7 gradients with many double bends on it. It is used by many people out driving and therefore can be busy with cars particularly at weekends. It is therefore necessary, when cycling, to take extreme care on the way down. Heed your speed, the road signs, and watch out for oncoming traffic. Remember, even when extreme care is taken, this road still makes an exhilarating ride.

Turn left at the Carron Bridge Hotel and continue over the Carron Bridge, built in 1695 to replace a ford which was for many hundreds of years part of the old drove road from Kilsyth to Stirling. This bridge looks larger than it needs to be, with its two span stone arches. This is because the river Carron was much larger before Loch Carron was dammed to make a reservoir.

Carry along this relatively flat minor road for 3 km to the top of the hill. At this point there is a car park with a picnic area offering a splendid view over almost the entire central belt of Scotland from Forth to Clyde. The descent now begins!

After descending for 3.5 km and having passed a road junction to the left look for a second junction which alas is not signposted. However its

INFORMATION

Distance: 30 km (18.75 miles) circular route.

Map: OS Landranger, sheet 64 & 65

Start and finish: Car park at the back of the public library, just off Duke Street, Denny.

Terrain: Many steep hills particularly on the first half. It is quite strenuous.

Refreshments: Places in Denny, Topps Farm, Carron Bridge Hotel and the Underwood Lockhouse on the Forth and Clyde Canal.

View from the Forth to the Clyde at the top of Tak-ma-doon road.

location can be identified, for it is by the first house on the left to be found bordering the road, on the outskirts of Kilsyth. Turn left here into Colzium Country Park and follow the road down towards Colzium House, passing en route the beautiful walled gardens and the Clock Theatre. Colzium House was formerly the nineteenth century seat of the Edmonstones of Duntreath and is now a museum worth a visit.

Commence along the main avenue of the park and leave by the main entrance on to the A803 just to the east of the small town of Kilsyth. Stay on this busy road for a very short distance leaving again at the first junction on the right, signposted for Dullatur.

Carry on along this road for 500 m to where a T-junction is reached and turn left. In turn follow this road for about a kilometre to where the Forth and Clyde Canal crosses under the road at Craigmarloch. Here join the tow path of the canal on the left and head off in an easterly direction.

Once on the canal tow path life is easy. For its 8.5 km of flat and peaceful cycling the first few kilometres are across the infamous Dullatur Bog. Dullatur bog was one of the most difficult obstacles encountered while constructing the canal. The land was very wet and soft and nothing could be built on it, because it would sink. Therefore it had to be completely drained. This caused great annoyance to the local inhabitants of Dullatur, because it disturbed millions of tiny toads displaced from their natural environment in the bog, thus sending them to invade the houses and lands of the people living round about.

Stone banks were then constructed which kept sinking into the ground. It was estimated that they sank to a depth of 50 feet below ground level in some places before they were consolidated, and could form the actual canal bank.

Swan on the Forth/Clyde canal.

A mural depicting the industrial heritage of Bonnybridge.

On now travelling east to Castlecary, passing the small village of Kelvinhead en route, which takes its name from the source of the river Kelvin in Dullatur Bog just to the south.Next past an obstacle on the canal route to Falkirk; that of the A80 Glasgow to Stirling Road where the canal uses a culvert under the road and which we can continue past with aid of a separate tunnel.

Here the first lock for 16 miles is to be found. This is called Wyndford lock, lock number 20.

A little further on to a hostelry. It's called the Underwood Lockhouse and, as its name suggests, the building was once the home of the lock-keeper. Commencing once again we quickly come to an aqueduct which takes us beneath the canal to Seabegs Wood. Here the Antonine Wall runs adjacent to the canal and at this point is very clearly defined. This is also is the site of a fortlet which was excavated in 1977, and is well worth a look!

It is now time to leave the canal and continue back on to the A803 via the footpath on the left. Once on the A803 cross it and continue into By-pass Road from where it links into Denny Road. Continue past Head of Muir for a kilometre to the junction of the A872 (Nethermains Road) and commence along this, finally retracing the route back to the car park in Denny.

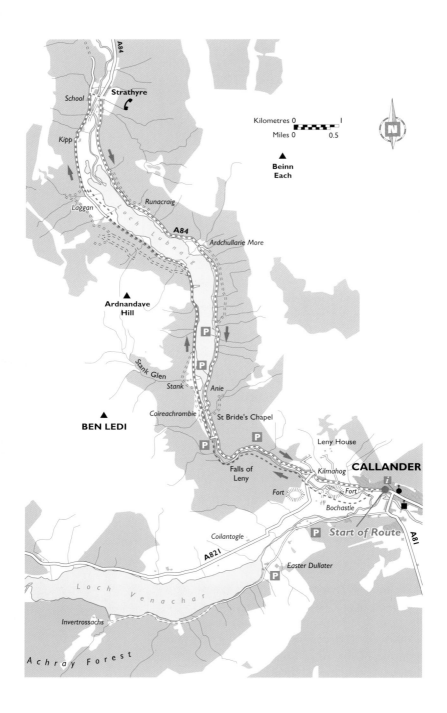

Kilometres 0 _____ 1
Miles 0 _____ 0.5

▲ Beinn Each

A84
Strathyre
School
Kipp
Runacraig
Laggan
A84
Ardchullarie More
Ardnandave Hill
Stank Glen
Stank
Anie
Coireachrombie
BEN LEDI
St Bride's Chapel
Leny House
CALLANDER
Kilmahog
Falls of Leny
Fort
Fort
Bochastle
Coilantogle
Start of Route
A821
Easter Dullater
A81
Loch Venachar
Invertrossachs
Achray Forest

CALLANDER TO STRATHYRE

This is probably the most straight forward route in the book for its length runs along a clearly defined cycle track. There is therefore no reason to describe, in any detail, the direction to be taken.

Begin on a path which starts at Leny Road (A84), Callander, 350 m to the west of the junction with Bridge Street (A81). On leaving the road descend the steep ramp, signposted for Strathyre, on to the track below. There is a railway signal reminding us that we will join the track bed of the dismantled Caledonian Railway further along the route. Commence along the track, negotiating the barriers erected to stop vehicles using it. After 1.5 km the track comes to the A821. Cross this road and recommence along the path on the other side.

Soon the noise of the torrent of the Garrb Uisge crashing down through the Falls of Leny can be heard and in one and half kilometres, they can be seen on the right-hand side of the track. At this point there are paths adjoining the track which can be taken to places close by to give a good view of the falls. These falls can be very spectacular at times, especially after heavy rain.

On the other bank of the river is the main road which goes through the Pass of Leny, the ancient gateway between the highlands and lowlands of Scotland. Through many centuries this pass had to be guarded. At Kilmahog there are remains of an iron age fort which guarded the Pass. The Romans too had a camp here for exactly the same purpose. The road, although now a modern construction, is on the line of the

INFORMATION

Distance: 15 km (9.37 miles) linear route. Or, a 27 km (16.87 miles) circular route see text.

Map: OS Landranger, sheet 57 and Explorer sheet 11. Part of this route is on Sustrans National Cycle Network route number 7, Inverness to Dover Map: 7c.

Start and finish: Car park to the south of Lennie Road.

Terrain: All off-road. Undulating but without steep hills; it is not difficult.

Refreshments: Places in Callander and Strathyre

The Falls of Leny.

old military road which took General Wade's English troops into the highlands to quell many rebellions by the highland clans against their rule.

After another kilometre the path opens on to a minor road with car parking facilities. This leads down to where there is a bridge across the river giving access to the Strathyre Holiday Cabins a little further on. This is also the point where a footpath begins to the summit of Ben Ledi. A little further along the track Loch Lubnaig opens out, and beyond to the north east Ben Vorlich's snow capped peak begins to emerge above the surrounding countryside. Carry along this track from where more and more of Ben Vorlich can be seen, until the mountain dominates the skyline to the east.

The author before commencing along the route to Ballquidder.

Soon another signpost is reached which indicates that Strathyre is only three miles (5 km) away. Here also the green and purple Forest Enterprise cycle signs can be seen pointing out the circular cycle track taking you further into the Strathyre Forest to come out again about 2 km further along our route. Then go on farther west to join yet another track once more leading into the forest.

The descent down to Laggen Farm Road now begins. This well-signposted route carries straight on at a junction (past a ford) then to the left and, next to the loch, joining the track bed of the dismantled railway. Carry along this track as it makes its way north along the banks of this wondrous loch with the white caps of the surrounding mountains pink in the morning sunlight and their wooded lower slopes green, blue, gold and brown shimmering in the crystal water. The stillness is disturbed only by a heron gliding over the surface of the water, occasionally dipping down below in its quest for a fish breakfast. It rises again to resume its vigil, leaving only V shaped ripples behind. After a kilometre the track, rough at this point, turns left once again and commences climbing steeply over a series of hairpin bends to another track high above.

From this track the descent into Strathyre begins. The track opens out to become the minor road serving the top of the village of Strathyre. Soon a junction is reached, turn right and cross the bridge spanning the River Balvag. Turn right on to the A84 where the small village of Strathyre has its centre.

You may prefer to return along the A84 Trunk Road, but as its name suggests this road is often very busy and there are stretches where the traffic moves very fast. There is not an abundance of space for the cyclist. However there are times when the road will be fairly quiet, and there are areas where there is a small running strip outside the white painted edge marking. You should therefore, depending on the conditions at the time, decide whether or not to use this road. I chose Sunday morning to cycle the route and decided, at that time, the road was safe enough to ride back to Callander.

View over Loch Lubnaig.

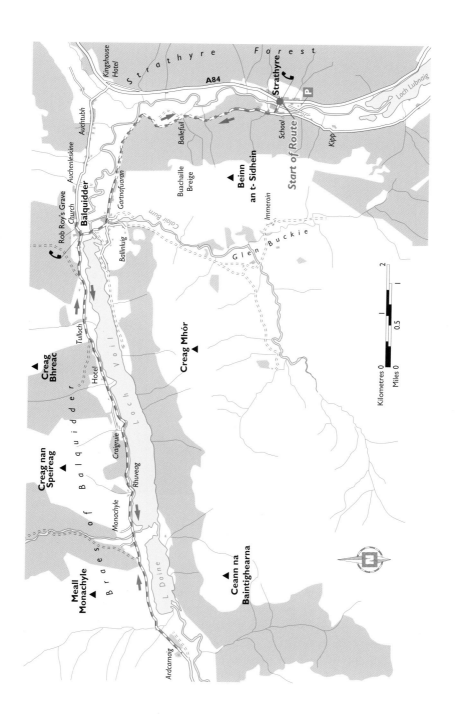

STRATHYRE TO BALQUHIDDER AND LOCH VOIL

The route begins at Bonnie Strathyre – to borrow the words of the famous song. Start on the minor road signposted for Stroneslaney and cross the bridge over the River Balvag, used in the last Route. Soon a T-junction is reached where a right turn is made still keeping on the Stroneslaney road. This single track road with passing places roughly follows the route of the River Balvag to its source in Loch Voil at Balquhidder. It first passes through part of a mature hardwood forest and then skirts along the remainder of this forest on the west side with open moor land to the east. There are a few road junctions on this stretch of road but they are connecting with forestry, or other tracks and should not cause any confusion. There is a good view over the Braes of Balquhidder from here.

After 3 km the little hamlet of Stroneslaney is reached. Thereafter the road continues for the same distance again into Balquhidder crossing, en route, the beautiful little masonry arch bridge over Calair Burn.

Just before entering Balquhidder there are two junctions in quick succession. Turn right at both of these. The road to the left at the second junction leads down to Stronvar Country House Hotel and Bygones Museum which is worth a visit. Cross over the River Balvag once again and enter the small village of Balquhidder.

There now follows a T-junction: a left turn will take you along the length of Loch Voil, a right turn to Balquhidder Parish Church. Turn to the right and follow the road along the short distance to the Parish Church. (We will come back to the left turn shortly.)

INFORMATION

Distance: 24 km (15 miles) linear route.

Map: OS Landranger, sheet 57 Explorer sheet 11. Part of this route is on Sustrans National Cycle Network route number 7, Inverness to Dover Map 7c.

Start and finish: Strathyre.

Terrain: Undulating but with a few steep hills. The worst is close to the beginning of the route on the minor road to Balquhidder. It is not particularly difficult.

Refreshments: Places in Strathyre, the Stronvar Country House Hotel and the Monachyle Mhor Hotel.

The old Kirk in Balquhidder with the new Kirk in the background.

For thousands of years people must have used this glen to travel across the country and in consequence there must have been a community here for just as long. William Wordsworth and his sister Dorothy visited Loch Voil in 1803, and it is said that after hearing a highland girl singing, he was moved to write his famous poem 'The Solitary Reaper'.

Reflections in Loch Voil

This area was shared by two clans the McLarens and the McGregors. The most famous McGregor was Rob Roy McGregor (1671 to 1734). He was a cattle dealer but how he came by some of the cattle is to say the least a little dubious. After becoming an outlaw, when hiding from the authorities deep within the Balquhidder Braes, he got caught up in the opposition to the Union of the Parliaments after 1707. He fought, from time to time on the side of James VII, to restore the Stuarts to the throne and was involved in the battle of Sheriffmuir. He became a folk hero and was immortalised by Sir Walter Scott in his famous novel *Rob Roy*. After such a tempestuous life he managed to die in his bed and is buried here in the old kirk yard along with his wife and two sons.

The Old Kirk now a ruin was built in 1631, on the site of a pre-reformation chapel alleged to have been visited by King James IV. The new Parish Church was built in 1853, and houses the early Christian St Angus stone and two interesting Gaelic bibles. Turn now retracing the short route back to the junction from where the road begins and runs along the length of Loch Voil.

Each loch in this area has its own characteristics and this one is no exception for it squeezes between the rocky crags of the hills, with the south side being particularly steep. These high hills reflect their abundance of colour beautifully on the surface of this narrow loch. This road is 9.5 km long. It passes the Monachyle Mhor Hotel at 3 km and continues to the end of Loch Voil at 6 km. It then skirts the much smaller Loch Doine, after which it continues for a further short distance before coming to an end. Just before the end of the road there is a picnic area where you can relax before retracing the same route back to Strathyre.

Sunset over the old Kirk.

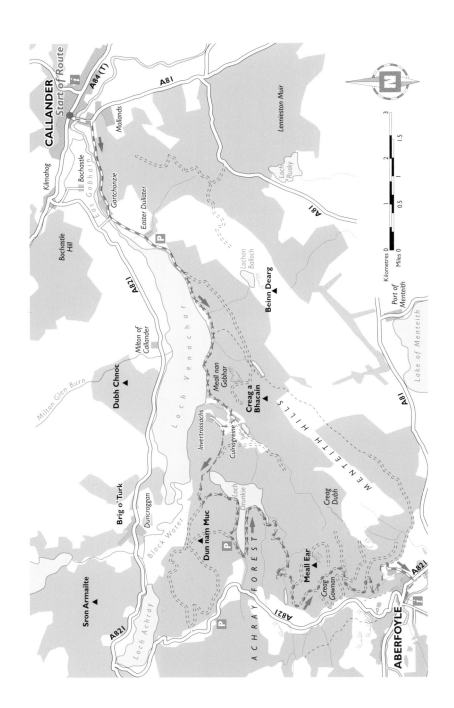

CALLANDER TO ABERFOYLE

Commence out of the car park past the mound of Tom-na-Chessaig referred to in Route 7 and turning right on to Bridge Street. Follow this road across the bridge which spans the river Teith and carry on to the Y-junction 200 m further on. Here turn right on to the road signposted for Invertrossachs and carry along for 400 m to a junction. Take the right fork and after some 2 km the banks of Loch Venachar are reached. This beautiful loch has an abundance of wildlife such as tufted duck, goosander, mute swan, common sand-piper, gray wagtail, buzzard, moor hen and

The author checks the route on the map at Loch Drunkie.

dippers. As you look down the length of the loch the mountainous panorama includes, from north to south Ben Ledi, Stuc Odhar, Ben Venue and the Menteith Hills.

Now the road continues for the next 4 km to hug the shore of the loch; as it does it begins to skirt the edge of Achray Forest. A short distance after Invertrossachs has been passed, a Y-junction on the road is reached. Look out for a green sign for cyclists pointing out that you should turn right, off the road. Go through a gate and commence along the Loch Venachar link which is a much narrower path.

Shortly after commencing along this path a junction is reached. Here take the right fork. The quality of this path varies: it's mostly fairly good but with the occasional soft spot. It is undulating as it continues alongside the steep bank of Loch Venachar.

INFORMATION

Distance: 21 km (13.12 miles) linear route.

Map: OS Landranger, sheet 57 Explorer sheet 11. Part of this route is on Sustrans National Cycle Network route number 7, Inverness to Dover Map 7c.

Start and finish: Car park to the south of Leny Road.

Terrain: Fairly flat over the first stage with a long uphill section in the middle, followed by a long and exhilarating descent into Aberfoyle. Almost all off-road.

Note: Within Loch Ard Forest there are stretches of road used by cars as a forest drive. These roads are often one way but cyclists can use them in either direction. However, look out for oncoming vehicles on both sides of the road.

Refreshments: Many places in Callander and Aberfoyle.

At the end of this small link track is a gate, taking cyclists through to the 3 m wide forest road which, like the smaller track, has a whin dust type finish. Turn left here and commence climbing through this large working forest. The forest is owned by Forest Enterprise who have kindly made some of the roads available for cycling. It is, therefore, important to keep to the roads marked by cycle signs. Achray Forest has mixture of species which includes some new scots pine, spruce and sitka spruce. Some of this forest is scheduled to be harvested in the year 2050.

After climbing for about a kilometre the road begins to descend. Midway through this descent a junction with another road is passed which if taken would eventually emerge on to the A821 just to the south of the access road to Loch Katrine. At the bottom of this hill at the place known as Larch Point, there are toilets and children's play and picnic areas.

The road now continues along the bonnie banks of Loch Drunkie lost under an array of colours which change with ever growing splendour from season to season. The loch is also the habitat of many varieties of duck including the mallard and often herons can be seen fishing at its edge.

The route meandering below.

After reaching the loch, the road turns and follows it once more, ascending along the length of one full side, sweeping round and then descending to the point where it leaves the banks and continues inland once again. At this point there is a road junction. Turn left around the head of the loch, to where the road now begins to climb over a distance of 2 km, which I hasten to add, is steeper than it looks. Over most of this length, the cyclist will find low gear will have to be engaged.

On this stretch the road passes several junctions. The first two are minor and it is clear which direction has to be taken to stay on route, at the third and fourth one must turn left both times. The route then comes to a four-way junction, where the direction of the route is clearly signposted. From here head straight on, and after a turn in the road a long and very welcome descent begins.

Loch Venachar with Ben Ledi in the background.

During the first stage of this descent the road passes close to the highest point in the forest which is called Meall Ear at a height of 333 m. The next junction is a T-junction at which point turn right. This is soon followed by a four-way junction at which you carry straight on. Midway down this stretch of road, a little way into the forest to the right, but visible from the road, is a beautiful waterfall, so slow down and look out for this for it is worth exploring. Turn right, almost through 180 degrees, at the next junction and continue this long and exhilarating descent.

This part of the route is close to The Queen Elizabeth Forest Park Visitor Centre and indeed any of the small paths hereabouts, on the right of the road, will take you there. However, you will have to walk for cycling on these narrow paths is, for obvious reason forbidden. Carry along this road as it bottoms out and even once again, for a short distance, climbing a little to where a sign clearly indicates that Aberfoyle is off to the right. Carry down this path over a little bridge, through Dounans Camp and continue for 200 m to the junction with the A821. Cross this road and commence along a footpath, which after a short distance finishes at the car park in the centre of Aberfoyle.

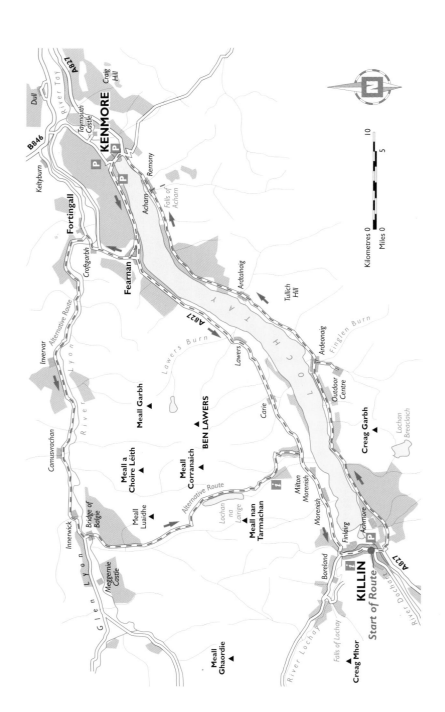

KILLIN TO KENMORE

Killin, at the western end of Loch Tay, is said to be the ancient burial place of Fingal one of Scotland's most famous warriors and there is a stone behind the village school which is alleged to mark his burial place. Even the name of this small town reflects this, for one school of thought is that the origin of the name Killin is derived from the Gaelic 'Cill Fhinn' meaning the burial place of Fingal. It is the ancient home of the Clans Campbell and MacNab, the latter being said to be directly descended from King Kenneth McAlpine.

The beautiful Falls of Dochart at the west end of the village is the place St Fillan performed many miracles and the reader can find out all about him and the history of the clans, in the Breadalbane Folklore Centre.

INFORMATION

Distance: 55 km (34.37 miles) circular route. This could also be a linear route for those who do not want to return from Kenmore to Killin via the A827.

Map: OS Landranger, sheet 51. Part of this route is on Sustrans National Cycle Network route number 7, Inverness to Dover Map 7c.

Start and finish: Car park opposite the Capercaillie Restaurant, Main Street ,Killin

Terrain: Generally undulating, with stretches of steep hills. The A827 can sometimes be busy with tourists, particularly in the height of summer.

Refreshments: Many Places in Killin and Kenmore also the Ardeonaig Hotel and the Coffee House, Croft na Caber.

Kenmore village church.

Falls of Dochart.

From the car park turn to the right on to Main Street and commence along past the Breadalbane Centre and across the bridge over the River Dochart, passing the beautiful Falls of Dochart as they cascade down through the rocks. After the bridge turn right and then immediately left on to the minor road which is signposted for Ardeonaig and South Loch Tay.

Once on this single track road Killin is soon left behind. The undulating road meanders between forest and open moor land, and after 2.5 km the first sight of the loch appears. Reflecting the splendour of the mountains surrounding it, the loch disappears behind another section of mature woodland.

At 4 km close to the point where the University of Edinburgh, Firbush Physical Education Centre is located the loch looms large. Follow alongside it now for 7 km, past Fiddlers Bay, to Ardeonaig where the hotel of the same name will supply refreshment if required. From here is a wonderful view across the loch to Ben Lawers: one of Scotland's highest mountains at 1214 m. (4046 feet). There is a road junction opposite the hotel where the road off to the right goes to Ardeonaig Outdoor Centre. However, the cycle route continues straight on.

After leaving Ardeonaig the road begins to climb over a fair distance and within this section there are some stretches of steep hill to negotiate. Once at the top of this hill there is an incredible view back over the loch to Killin and beyond to Glen Lochay.

The road then descends slightly over the next kilometre rising over a short distance before descending steeply into Ardtainaig. This road is very good for cycling with a good surface and just enough ups and downs to make it interesting.

This area must have had a fair amount of people living in it at one time for at regular intervals along the road there are a number of derelict and ruined cottages.

After Ardtainaig the road rises once again over the next 5 km to where the first glimpse of the beautiful village of Kenmore at the eastern end of the loch is seen. The road now begins to descend and after a short distance the small village of Acharn is reached. There is a road off to the right to the spectacular Falls of Acharn. Next to the falls there is a cave once visited by Robert Burns who, referring to its likely use in ancient times, called it the Hermit's Mossy Cell.

Continue on the route to Croft na Caber where there is a hotel, chalet complex and water sports centre. There is also a coffee house and cafe where, once again, refreshment can be had if required.

This is also the site of the Scottish Crannog Centre. A crannog is an ancient loch dwelling built off-shore using a series of timber piles around a mound of stones sunk onto the bed of the loch, which was repeated until a stony island appeared above the surface of the loch. The timber round house and external circular causeway was then built on these piles. A causeway to the shore was also built with a portion that could be lifted for security purposes. This was a very secure construction that gave protection against wild animals and invaders. There are 18 Crannogs in Loch Tay and archaeologists, mainly from the University of Edinburgh, have been excavating them for years. They have now reconstructed a complete Crannog using the building methods of 2000 years ago, which is the first project of this kind. The Crannog is open to the public with a temporary onshore exhibition featuring a video of the underwater crannog excavations and many ancient discoveries including a long boat. Later it is hoped to build a permanent visitor centre. Seeing this wonderful piece of living history must not be missed.

Carry on along the last kilometre to the junction with the A827, en route you will see Spry Island, the largest crannog in the loch.

Turn left at the junction onto the road signposted to Killin and almost immediately enter the beautiful village of Kenmore. It is important to point out that I have chosen the A827 as the second half of this route because I feel it is safe enough to be used for cycling. However it's up to you to decide, depending on the conditions and your ability, whether or not to use this road or to return by retracing the route taken on the first half.

Kenmore was once visited by Queen Victoria and Prince Albert who stayed at Taymouth Castle with the Marquis of Breadalbane. The Queen, who was very fond of Scotland, was said to have been enthralled by the village and countryside around. The castle is now a school and the grounds are a golf course.

The A827, not surprisingly is similar in terrain as the road on the other side of the loch. It is however less wooded and therefore gives a more sustained view of the loch and its surrounding mountains.

After 5.5 km. a road junction is reached. Here the road to the right heads north into Glen Lyon passing to the north of Ben Lawers and then returning back to the A827 about 14 km to the west, passing en route the Ben Lawers Visitor Centre. Although this adds an extra 20 km and a lot more hills to the journey it is a very interesting and picturesque route.

Carry along the A827 to Lawers where a splendid view over the mountains to the south, including Ben Vorlich, can be had. Here another refreshment stop can be made at the Inn, before carrying on the remaining 13 km back to Killin.

The Scottish Crannog Centre at Loch Tay.

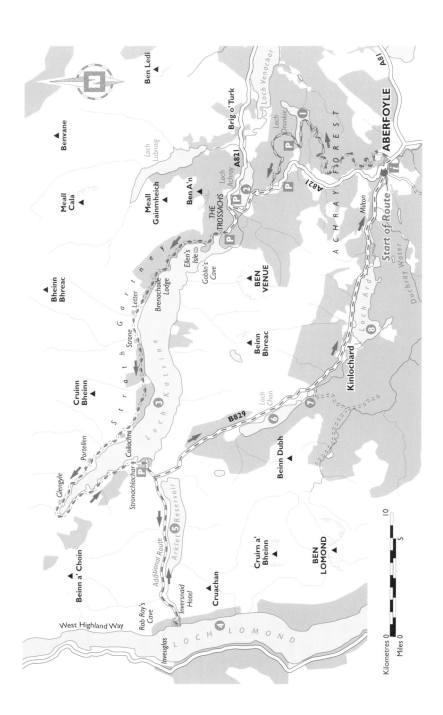

ABERFOYLE TO LOCH KATRINE
(THE TOUR OF EIGHT LOCHS)

Aberfoyle was known to have worked Iron Ore and records of this go back as far as the fifteenth century. It is said, at this time the famous sword-maker Andreas Ferrara made his highly sought after weapons in this district. More recently slate has been quarried around the district.

As with its neighbour to the north, Callander, this village has been occupied with tourism since the end of the eighteenth century. Today, this vibrant village is extremely busy all year round with tourists anxious to take in all the beauties of the Trossachs.

The route begins at the public car park close to the Scottish Woollen Mill. Commence to the east end of this car park and join the path along the track bed of the dismantled railway line. At the end of this path cross the A821 onto a minor road. This road is recognised by a large black and white sign which advertises Dounan's Outdoor Centre. Commence up this road to Dounan's Camp. Continue straight through the camp and turn left at the T-junction with a 3 m wide forest road. Follow this road as it climbs steeply uphill for 5 km, through Achray Forest. Since there is a fuller description of this forest in Route 15, I will confine the narrative to a brief description of the route with distances measured from the point that the forest road was reached.

At the first junction, after one kilometre turn left at an acute angle, leading to a four-way junction, at 1.75 km where you carry straight on. Next there's a T-junction at 3 km turn left. Carry on now for 2 km to the next four-way junction and carry straight on. At this point the climb is thankfully over and the road now begins to make a long slow descent. The next junction is at 5.5 km, where a right turn is made. This is

INFORMATION

Distance: 62 km (38.75) circular route.

Map: OS Landranger, sheet 56 & 57 Explorer sheet 11. Part of this route is on Sustrans National Cycle Network route number 7, Inverness to Dover Map 7c.

Start and finish: Car park at the Scottish Woollen Mill Aberfoyle.

Terrain: Very hilly, particularly on the first stage over the Dukes Pass. However, it is better to get the worst over at the beginning. Thereafter it is undulating with short stretches of steep gradient. This route will take the average person most of a day. I do not recommend it for children.

Refreshments: Many places in Aberfoyle, the Visitor Centre Loch Katrine and Altskeith Hotel Kinlochard.

The author admiring the view along the route.

followed 100 m farther on by another right turn.
Follow the road for a further one kilometre and carry
straight on veering to the left. Yet another kilometre
is travelled, at which point turn left and in 500 m
turn right along the banks of Loch Drunkie, the first
of the lochs. The next junction is found 2 km
further on, where a left turn is made. It should be
noted here that in this stretch of road there are

toilets and a children's
play area. There are also
many picnic sites here
abouts. The junction
just referred to is where
the route deviates from
the route to Callander.
Once the left turn has
been made the cyclist is
now heading for Loch
Katrine.

A distant view of Ben
Lomond.

Follow this road for 500 m at which point carry
straight on for a similar distance to aT-junction
and turn right. Within a few metres there's another
T-junction where a left turn is made. Again, in 200
m or so another T-junction is reached and here
veer to the left. Carry on now for 2 km passing one
junction en route to aT-junction where a left turn
is made. After another 500 m a four-way junction is
reached. Here turn left and follow the forest road
the final few metres to the junction with the A821
and turn right. Here looking east there is a good
view of Loch Achray, the second loch on the tour.
Take this road for 2 km to where the brown tourist
sign points to a left turn for Loch Katrine.

Turn onto the access road to, the third loch, Loch
Katrine, which is still technically the A821. Carry
along this road for 1.5 km to its end at the pier
where the steamer, the Sir Walter Scott, sails to
and from Stonachlachar several times a day all
summer long.

The Sir Walter Scott was built in Dumbarton by
William Denny and Bros. Ltd and brought up in

sections, first by barge along the river Leven and across Loch Lomond to Inversnaid and then she continued her journey by horse and cart to Stonachlachar where she was assembled on the loch. Launched in 1899, she is the only steam screw passenger ship still in service in Scotland.

Since the middle of 19th century Loch Katrine has been the source of Glasgow's water supply.

Points of interest around Loch Katrine are too numerous to mention in this book. However, on the way there are information boards describing each area either historically, geographically, or its significance in folklore.

The Sir Walter Scott on Loch Katrine.

The perimeter road is undulating as it follows the contours of the hard rocky edge of the loch. In some areas the hills are quite prolonged and steep. The perimeter road is private but walking and cycling are allowed and encouraged. There are no unauthorised motor vehicles allowed on this road, but never the less, this road is used by West of Scotland Water vehicles and other vehicles belonging to residents around the loch. In my experience the drivers of these vehicles are very careful and mindful of the many walkers and cyclists who use this road, but please take care and keep in control at all times.

Commence along this road for one kilometre to Allt na Cailliche, the Witches Burn which enters the loch at Murlaggan Bay: the bag shaped bay on the opposite shore. These are two place names which give insight into the culture of the area. One descriptive the other connected with the alleged devil worshipping of the inhabitants in former times.

Loch Katrine is fed by many burns rather than one great river, a feature that attracted the City Engineers in the nineteenth century in their search for a pure supply of Glasgow's water. This water was also the main element of a flourishing illicit industry, whisky distilling. The smuggling of this very popular product was well organised in spite of the presence in numbers of Gaugers or Excise men. Specialist gangs of men would pick up the contraband from the many still operators and transport it by pack horse to Drymen and Glasgow. These groups adopted mock official titles such as THE ROYAL DEFIANCE BLADDER BAND. Godgers Pass is above Glasahoile on the opposite shore of the loch.

After travelling on for a bit further look out to Eilean Molach – the rough island or Ellan's Island, with its dense and twisted vegetation – where a famous incident took place. An English soldier swimming over to question a group of women and children who were taking refuge there was beheaded by a single blow from Ellan Stewart whose name became linked with the Island. The women and children were McGregors and the brave action of the woman may have inspired the stern character of Helen the wife of Rob Roy in Sir Walter Scott's novel. Scott also used a version of the event in 'The Lady of the Lake'. Scott describes, the woman's heroic defence : 'Behind an Oak I saw her stand a naked dirk gleamed in her hand.' The Lady of the Lake in the poem was the young heroine, the fair Ellan who sailed from the island to the bay below this point to silver strand with its pebbles bright as snow.

On now past many more points of interest to Portnellan the burial ground of the clan McGregor. When the level of the loch was to be raised this burial ground would have been submerged so it was decided to move it to its present location.

Continue along the short distance past Glengyle House, the birth place of the notorious Rob Roy

McGregor, to where the head of the loch is reached. The road turns from west to east. It then continues along the south bank of the loch for the remaining 4 km to Stonachlachar.

Once Stonachlachar has been reached continue to follow the road inland to where there is a gate back on to the public road. After this gate, turn left if you wish to go down to the pier where the Sir Walter Scott comes in, or carry straight on, if you wish to remain on the route. It's uphill very steeply for 500m to the road junction with the B829. At this point it is only a 6 km diversion to Inversnaid on beautiful Loch Lomond. The route however, turns left and follows the B829 back to Aberfoyle some 17.5 km to the south east. From here the road is similar to that taken around Loch Katrine, generally undulating with some steep hills.

Before beginning the last leg of this journey, pause to look over the fifth loch in our tour. This is the beautiful Loch Arklet, another loch which supplies the City of Glasgow with water. It is flanked on both sides by majestic mountains.

Once on this road it's uphill again, this time for 2 km passing a sign for a cattle grid. However, the grid itself has recently been removed and the road filled in.

Pass now the sixth loch on this route which is Loch Chon followed immediately by number seven, the tiny Loch Dhu and carry on into Kinlochard on the last loch, the splendid Loch Ard with its water sports centre. At the east end of this little village is the Altskeith Hotel where well earned sustenance can be had.

Continue on now the remaining 8 km, passing en route the little village of Milton, back to Aberfoyle.

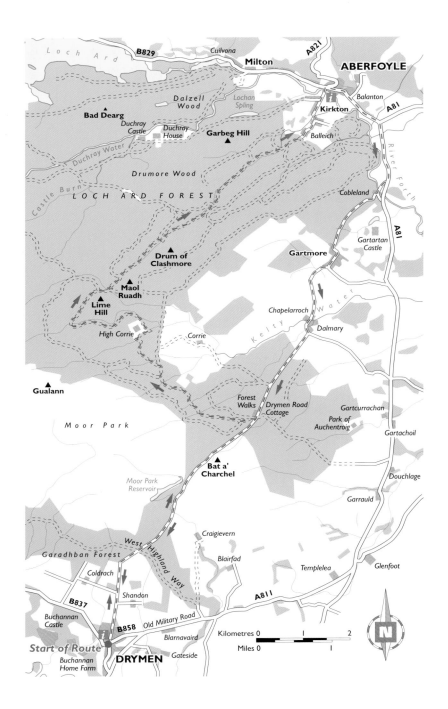

DRYMEN TO ABERFOYLE

The small, but picturesque, village of Drymen is a busy place throughout the year, particularly at weekends and holidays for it is one of the most popular destinations for local people out on an afternoon cycle ride, walk or drive.

The name of Drymen is of Celtic origin and means ridge or knoll describing the physical features of the land around the district. The village itself is very old with records of a church being in existence there as far back as 1248. Throughout its long history Drymen has been home to those people who worked the lands belonging to the Duke of Montrose, the owner of most of the lands around the district.

The route begins in the centre of Drymen at the village green, known as the Square, from where we head north past the road to Stirling (B858) on to the Old Gartmore Road. Once past Drymen Primary School open country is soon reached where the road becomes single track with passing places. The road begins to ascend at a manageable incline into Garadhban Forest. The view over to the east from the Menteith Hills to the Gargunnock Hills is most atmospheric. Dependent on the weather it can look angry and awe inspiring or tranquil and benign, but certainly always beautiful.

After 2 km the road begins to ascend more steeply as it reaches the forest where the West Highland Way, which runs at right angles to the road, is crossed. After this crossing continue for another 2 km back out on to open countryside and past Muir Park Reservoir on the left and on into the Loch Ard Forest. At 6.5 km an extensive five-way junction is reached about 200 m before Drymen Road Cottage. From this point the instructions have to be fairly comprehensive for there is a myriad of tracks in this forest. At this junction bear

INFORMATION

Distance: 30 km (18.75 miles) circular route.

Map: OS Landranger, sheet 57. This route is part of Sustrans National Cycle Network route number 7 Inverness to Dover Map 7c.

Start and finish: The centre of Drymen at the village green.

Terrain: Generally undulating, with some steep hills prolonged at times.

Refreshments: Places in Drymen, Aberfoyle and the Black Bull in Gartmore.

hard left for a few metres almost turning back on yourself. Now follow this forest track for half a kilometre, to the first Y-junction. Take the right fork and continue on for almost 2 km to another Y-junction where the right fork is taken again. After a very short distance of about 300 m yet another Y-junction is reached. At this point turn left and carry along this track for one kilometre to the T-junction at High Corrie and turn right. Then fairly quickly, turn left at the next junction and follow the road as it follows Corrie burn and then meanders around Lime Hill. At the next junction take the right fork and then shortly after crossing the Keltie Water another junction is reached where a left turn is made. Continue for about a kilometre on this stretch of road passing one junction on the left. After this a Y-junction is reached where the left fork is taken. On now for almost a kilometre, to another Y junction, where this time the right fork is taken. Carry on now for the remaining 5.5 km, straight over a four-way junction, on this road into Aberfoyle, neither turning left nor right.

Once Aberfoyle has been reached look out for the Kirkton Church Yard where as the information board at the gate explains there are many stories. On either side of the front entrance to this now ruined church are two Mort Safes. These look like iron coffins and were used at the time of the body snatchers to protect the recently dead. The heavy Mort Safe was placed on top of the coffin inside the grave for six weeks then it was removed and the grave was infilled.

Carry on across the bridge over the river Forth and turn right into the car park a few metres before Main Street is reached. Head straight through this car park to its western end where a path continues alongside the A821. Once this path terminates continue along the A821 for 3 km. passing en route the junction with the A81, to the minor road on the right signposted to Gartmore.

A mortsafe in Kirkton Churchyard.

The minor road to Gartmore and beyond is, as you may have no doubt learned to expect, undulating with stretches of steeper inclines. After crossing the bridge over the river Forth a Y-junction is reached. Here take the right fork, and the road then climbs fairly steeply before descending into the planned village of Gartmore. Once the outskirts of the village is reached the road turns at right angles and continues for 200 m before turning again at right angles into the main street. At this second turning is the entrance to the Gartmore Estate with its rather flamboyant gate visible about 100m further on. This is where the Cunningham Memorial can be found a few metres along a path to the left of the gateway.

Robert Bontine Cunningham Graham lived between 1832 and 1936. His memorial declares that he was a famous author, traveller, horseman, patriotic Scot who died in Argentina and was buried on the island of Inchmahome on the Lake of Menteith. Graham who could claim descent from the Stewart Kings, was known as Don Roberto

Countryside around Gartmore.

Hazy wintry sunset.

because of the time he spent in Latin America. He was however, best known in Scotland as an champion of the working class. Having first become the Liberal member of Parliament for North West Lanarkshire between 1886 to 1892. He fought for the reduction of the working day and the need to nationalise key industries. He also supported Irish Home Rule. He became the first president of the Scottish Labour Party in 1888 which was a forerunner of the Labour Party. He was president of the Scottish National Party from its formation in 1934 until his death.

On returning to the route commence down through the beautiful little village of Gartmore with the Black Bull Hotel on the left where refreshment can be had. Gartmore village is a fine example of a planned estate village built to provide homes for the estate workers on Gartmore Estate.

At the bottom of the village street turn right and follow the road for half a kilometre to where there is a Y-junction and turn left. After this there is a long downhill stretch to the old stone bridge over the Keltie Water.

Just after crossing the Keltie Water a Y-junction is reached. At this point turn right and follow the signpost to Drymen. Commence along this road climbing slowly to Drymen Road Cottage after which the hill ascends steeply for 200 m to the junction. Here join the road taken over the first 6.5 km of the route and retrace it back to Drymen, with its beautiful views over Loch Lomond still to be enjoyed.

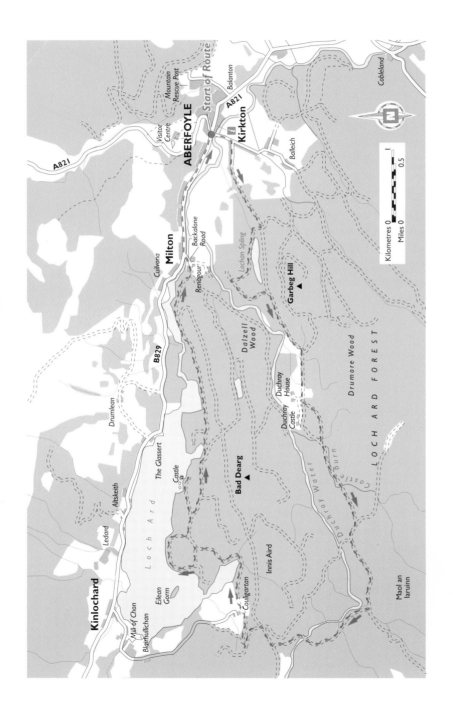

Start of Route

ABERFOYLE

Kirkton

A821

A821

A821

B829

Balanton

Cobleland

Balleich

Visitor Centre

Mountain Rescue Post

Milton

Culuona

Backalone Road

Renagour

Lochan Spling

Garbeg Hill ▲

Dalzell Wood

Drumore Wood

Duchray House

Duchray Castle

Duchray Water

Castle Burn

LOCH ARD FOREST

Drumlean

The Glassert

Castle

Bad Dearg ▲

Innis Aird

Maol an Iaruinn

Kinlochard

Ledard

Altskeith

Loch Ard

Eilean Gorm

Mill of Chon

Blairhullichan

Couligartan

Kilometres 0

Miles 0

0.5

THE LOCH ARD CIRCLE

The route begins at the car park, just off Main Road, Aberfoyle. Head to the west end of this car park and turn left into Manse Road. Commence across the bridge over the river Forth and after a short distance turn right and travel uphill past the Covenanters Inn. A little way past this hotel open country is reached and it is not far to the beginning of Loch Ard Forest. After about a kilometre.a four-way junction is reached. Here leave the main track and turn right on to a much narrower path which is marked by a blue, Forest Enterprise, cycle sign and commence down a slight gradient and begin to skirt the edge of Lochan Spling. After about a kilometre. a junction is reached. Turn left, continuing along this undulating path back to the junction with the main track once again. Turn right passing a picnic area known as Gartnaul before coming to a junction with the private road to Duchray House. Here turn left following the cycle sign.

This estate includes Duchray Castle on the south bank of Duchray Water, built by the Graham's of Downie at the end of the sixteenth century. Alas this castle cannot be seen from the track. The castle was the gathering place of a troop raised on behalf of the ninth Earl of Glencairn in 1653, to support the restoration of the Stuart Monarchy. A few days later they defeated a detachment of Cromwell's Army near Aberfoyle.

Continue along this undulating road through this working forest, so be careful of any forestry vehicles which may also be using the track. At the next T-junction carry straight on. There follows a

INFORMATION

Distance: 19 km (11.87 miles) circular route.

Map: OS Landranger, sheet 57 Explorer sheet 11.

Start and finish: The centre of Aberfoyle.

Terrain: The route is generally undulating, with some short stretches of steep hills.

Refreshments: Places in Aberfoyle. I recommend a picnic is taken.

Greag-Bheuthe from Aberfoyle.

junction with a road to the right with a bridge over a burn. This is also an access road into Duchray Estate so ignore it and stay on the main track. Continue along this main forest avenue for 2 km to where a cottage is located.

There is a track off to the right continuing down a hill to an aqueduct at the bottom. This is the aqueduct which carries Glasgow's water supply from Loch Katrine to the reservoirs in Milngavie. Continue past this track again keeping to the main forest avenue for another kilometre at which point turn right following once more a cycle sign, this time a green one. The following hill although not arduous, is the steepest that will be encountered on this route. The track now runs parallel to Duchray Water for about a kilometre and here among the trees Black Linn of Blairvaich (Waterfall) is located and although it cannot be seen from the track, it certainly can be heard. The path to the Linn is found at the bridge over the river soon to be crossed. A short distance further on, the track opens out into an area where the forest has been harvested leaving the moorland empty with its criss-cross of trenches looking something like a war zone. Cross the Duchray Water by a fairly recently constructed bridge and continue on the other side to a T-junction. Turn right following yet another cycle sign. Carry on uphill passing underneath another aqueduct carrying Glasgow's water supply high over the valley below.

At the top of this hill there is a three-way junction. Here turn to the left following a red cycle sign and commence downhill towards Couligarten. At the first junction located on this stretch of road take the right fork: there soon follows a four-way junction. Here turn right and go along the track which for the most part meanders along the south bank of the beautiful Loch Ard.

After 2 km a little diversion can be taken by turning left and following this track as it continues alongside the loch passing as it does a Crannog and the little Island of Eilean Gorm. Once back to the main track turn left and after about 500 m there is another junction. Here take the right fork. If however, you take the left track which once

Ruins of Duke Murdochs Castle on Eilean Gorm.

more follows the banks of the loch to come to an end after about 500 m, four small islands can be seen just off-shore. On the most easterly of these islands stands the ruins of Duke Murdoch's Castle which was built by Murdoch Stewart, the Duke of Albany (1362 to 1425). After spending some years as a prisoner in England along with King James I, Murdoch was released and returned to Scotland, to succeed his father as Regent of Scotland whilst James still remained a prisoner. However he lacked the capacity to carry out this task effectively and when James I eventually returned to Scotland, he had him executed for perpetrating acts of bad government, and his estates were forfeit.

On returning back to the main track continue for another 3 km keeping close to the loch until a gate

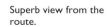

Superb view from the route.

is reached. Pass through this gate and continue past some cottages to a road junction. Now in Milton, turn left and follow this road down to the B829 and turn right. Commence along this road for just over a kilometre back to Aberfoyle. Turn right into Manse Road and then quickly left back into the car park from where the route began.

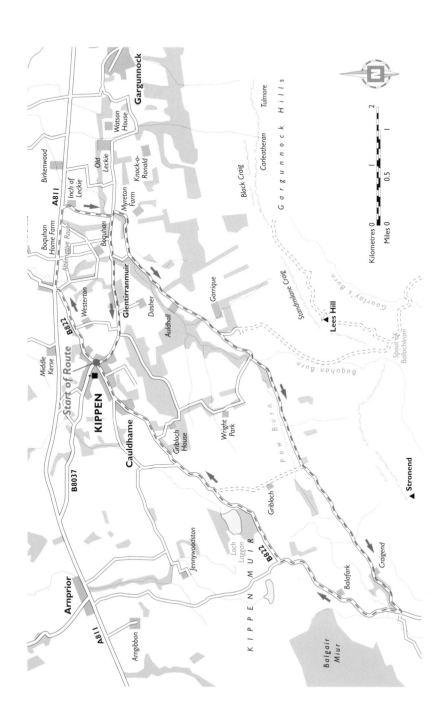

KIPPEN TO KIPPEN MUIR

Kippin is a small picturesque village serving the needs of the local agricultural population around. It has remained virtually unchanged over the last two centuries and still retains its charm. It has, like many others around these parts been a place for tourism. Indeed, it was a favourite place for people from Glasgow. There was an eighteenth century building in the village known as Tailor's Building, now demolished, which was divided into two room flats each with a box bed. During the Glasgow Fair the guests slept in shifts and it was known locally as the jail. There has been a church and a settlement in Kippen since 1238. All that is left of the old parish church in the old graveyard at the end of the Cross, is the west gable and the belfry. This church was rebuilt in 1691 from an earlier one on the same site.

The route begins at the war memorial cross in Kippen, almost outside the Cross Keys Hotel. Turn right into Burnside and carry along it out of the village, where you get a glimpse of the Wallace Monument some distance away to the east with the Ochil Hills behind. This road although now not complete is part of the centuries old Kings Highway, as described in the Gargunnock Chapter of the *Third Statistical Account of Stirling and Clackmannan*, once the main road to Stirling. After a kilometre this minor road ends at a yard. Commence through this, for it is a right of way, to a track on the other side and take this to a junction with a small path and go along it. After a short distance between dense woodland a farm gate is reached. Hoist your bicycle over this gate and enter the field on the other side via the adjacent kissing gate. Carry on through this small field on foot to where an old gate is located. Go through this gate remembering to close it again after you, unless you found it open. Once through the gate remount and take the track on the other side across the bridge

INFORMATION

Distance: 20 km (12.5 miles) circular route.

Map: OS Landranger, sheet 57.

Start and finish: The centre of Kippen.

Terrain: Generally undulating, with some steep hills, prolonged at times.

Refreshments:. Places in Kippen. It should be noted that there is no place to have any refreshment except were the route starts and finishes. Therefore I suggest that a picnic is taken.

View over Loch Laggan.

over Boquhan Burn and carry on. The beautiful mansion to be seen on the left is Boquhan House.

The road then passes a barn and continues for about 600 m to a road junction with a minor road. An alternative route to this junction is to leave by the B822 to the north east and head downhill to the junction with the A811 and turning right towards Stirling. Take care on this busy road for the traffic is fast moving. Carry along this road for a kilometre. to the junction of a minor road on the right. This can be recognised by the sign for Inch of Leckie. Turn into this road and commence uphill to where the road turns at right angles. It is here that these two alternative routes merge.

Carry along this minor road past an interesting red sandstone cottage to where the road once again turns at right angles. After a kilometre the entrance to Fourmerk Farm is past. As the ancient currency of Scotland was the merk it may be possible to deduce that many centuries ago this farm cost four merks to rent.

The road continues to undulate with some short lengths of steep hill as it meanders past beautiful river valleys and through agricultural land. The Gargunnock Hills tower overhead, for about a kilometre. The route begins to ascend much more steeply for yet another kilometre. Cross the bridge over the Pow Burn and continue along this wonderfully tranquil road where, in the fields, sheep and pheasants mingle happily together. There is a wonderful sense of peace on this road, a feeling of timelessness and of being many miles away from everything.

Continue to ascend now to where there is a stock gate across the road. This is the first of three such gates and it is of the utmost importance to close these gates behind you after passing through. The road now crosses open grazing land so look out for sheep on it and take care not to frighten them.

The road now begins its descent past, on the southside, Lees Hill and Stronend which are part of the Fintry Hills. There are little patchworks of forest on the lower ground to the north and peeping out from one of them can be seen the top of Ben Lomond.

A pastoral scene with mountains in splendour behind.

Continue to descend to the four-way junction with the B822 and turn right here. It may be interesting to note that the road straight across is part of another route featured in *25 Cycle Routes in and around Glasgow.*

From the four-way junction turn right on to the B822 and after a short distance the road starts to ascend through moorland with Kippen Muir on the left. The road climbs constantly with varying gradients for 2.5 km,.during which there are more fleeting glimpses of Ben Lomond. Once the summit of this long gradient has been reached, at the point where the junction with the minor road to Arnprior is located, there is a spectacular panoramic view over the mountains of the Trossachs to the north, and Ben Lomond and the Arrochar Alps to the west, and with the flat Flanders Moss situated directly below.

Continue now for another 1.5 km, still staying on the undulating B822, to Loch Laggan with its vast array of different species of water fowl. Soon after this the road begins its descent with the beautiful views continuing to enthral as you glide effortlessly downhill into Kippen. The route enters the village on Fintry Road with its beautiful whitewashed cottages and winds its way into Main Street, back to the cross where this mentally and physically stimulating route ends.

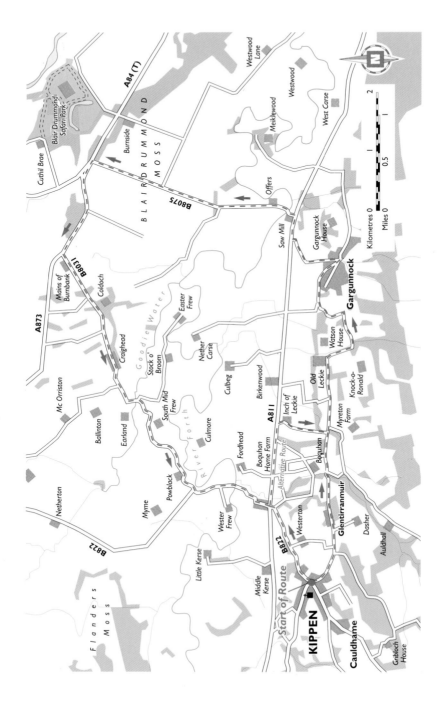

KIPPEN TO GARGUNNOCK

The route starts from the same place as the previous route and has the same alternative route if required. It begins at the war memorial cross in Kippen, almost outside the Cross Keys Hotel. Turn right into Burnside and carry along it out of the village, where you get a glimpse of the Wallace Monument some distance away to the east with the Ochil Hills behind. This road although now not complete is part of the centuries old Kings Highway, as described in the Gargunnock Chapter of the *Third Statistical Account of Stirling and Clackmannan*, once the main road to Stirling. After a kilometre this minor road ends at a yard. Commence through this, for it is a right of way, to a track on the other side and take this to a junction with a small path and go along it. After a short distance between dense woodland a farm gate is reached. Hoist your bicycle over this gate and enter the field on the other side via the adjacent kissing gate. Carry on through this small field on foot to where an old gate is located. Go through this gate remembering to close it again after you, unless you found it open. Once through the gate remount and take the track on the other side across the bridge over Boquhan Burn and carry on. The beautiful mansion to be seen on the left is Boquhan House.

INFORMATION

Distance: 21 km (13.12 miles) circular route.

Map: OS Landranger, sheet 57.

Start and finish: The centre of Kippen.

Terrain: Generally flat, with one uphill stretch over the last kilometre. The busy A811 has to be crossed twice.

Refreshments: Places in Kippen and Gargunnock.

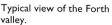
Typical view of the Forth valley.

The road then passes a barn and continues for about 600 m to a road junction with a minor road. An alternative route to this junction is to leave by the B822 to the north east and head downhill to the junction with the A811 and turning right towards Stirling. Take care on this busy road for the traffic is fast moving. Carry along this road for a kilometre. to the junction of a minor road on the right. This can be recognised by the sign for Inch of Leckie. Turn into this road and commence uphill to where the road turns at right angles. It is here that these two alternative routes merge.

Village scene.

Carry along this minor road past an interesting red sandstone cottage for only a few metres to where the track now continues straight on. Take this track as it passes houses on the left and continue, turning hard right past the remains of Old Leckie Castle, for 1.75 km to a T-junction and turn left on to a minor road. Carry on for a kilometre to another junction and turn right and follow this road, known as Leckie Road, the short distance into the village of Gargunnock with its splendid backdrop of the Gargunnock Hills .

There has probably been a settlement at Gargunnock from prehistoric times although the earliest recording is through an excavation made in the area in the 1950s where a dwelling house was unearthed and dated from the first century AD. Some of the remains from this excavation can be seen at the Museum of Antiquities in Edinburgh.

During the War of Independence William Wallace descended from his hiding place in the Gargunnock Hills, at the request of the local people, to rout the English Garrison of Peel of Gargunnock who had, for some time, been terrorising them. Charles Edward Stuart (Bonnie Price Charlie) marched with his troops through the parish in September 1745 and had dinner at Old Leckie Castle.

Gargunnock was once known for basket weaving; an industry which has long since died out. Today the village, still a quiet and pleasant place, has had its outskirts

enlarged somewhat by people who work predominantly in
Stirling some 6.5 km. to the east.

When the Square is reached, you'll see it's a four-
way junction. Turn left along Station Road, which
after 1.5 km reaches the A811. Here turn right
following the signs for Stirling and very quickly
take the B8075 signposted for Doune.

Commence along this road soon crossing the bridge
spanning the River Forth and on across the flat
lands, or Carse, of Flanders Moss and Drip Moss
until the junction of the A84 Trunk Road.
According to the *First Statistical Account* of this
area the author states that the Carse was once
under the sea surrounded by high hills to both the
north and south, and that at a later date it was
covered by forest of mainly oak. It is alleged that
this forest was cut down during the Roman
occupation.

It is interesting to see the contrast between these
flat lands and the mountains beyond that
completely dominate the horizon.

Turn left and within several metres the
access road linking the Trunk Road with
the A873 is reached. Close to this point is
Blair Drummond Safari Leisure Park, and
its magnificent array of wild animals can
be seen roaming freely. These include a
pride of lions, Siberian tigers, elephants
from Zimbabwe, and many more.

Take this road, signposted for Thornhill
and Aberfoyle, and continue along it for 2

A fine specimen of a lion
in Blair Drummond Safari
Leisure Park.

km to the B8031, turning left at the signpost for
Kippen. Carry along this meandering road around
some double bends to the junction of the B822.
Turn left and cross the River Forth once again
before coming to the junction of the A811.

Here cross this busy road and commence up the hill
on the B822 for the last 1.5 km back to Kippen.

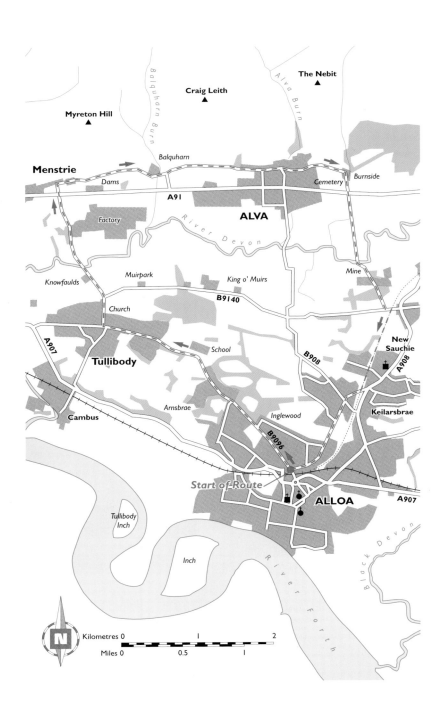

ALLOA TO ALVA

Alloa is an ancient town mentioned in the Royal Charter of 1398 bestowing it to Sir Thomas Erskine by King Robert III. Like many other parts of the County of Clackmannan, Alloa is renowned for its woollen industry which fortunately still thrives today. Beer has been brewed in Alloa since 1645 and at one time the town was famous for its ship building industry.

The route starts at the car park, on to Tullibody Road for 3 km into the village of Tullibody, travelling gradually uphill for the first two kilometres and then descending for the third where it changes name to Alloa Road.

Tullibody is even older than its near neighbour Alloa being able to trace its foundation back to the reign of Kenneth McAlpine in the ninth century.

On reaching the four-way junction of Stirling Road in the west, Alloa Road in the east, Main Street in the south and Menstrie Road to the north, turn right into Menstrie Road and continue for 500 m to a Y-junction. Take the left fork which is the continuation of Menstrie Road. Carry on down this road to the junction with the A91 and taking care crossing this busy road. Carry straight on over this road and continue, still on Menstrie Road, to the T-junction a short distance further on.

On reaching the A91 however, you may wish to investigate Menstrie Castle which necessitates turning left and following the signs to where it is located in Menstrie Place.

Menstrie Castle is a restored sixteenth century town house, the birthplace of Sir William Alexander the first Earl of Stirling, in 1567. Alexander was the founder of the ill-fated Scottish Colony of Nova Scotia. Charles I awarded 45 baronets of Nova Scotia in consideration for

INFORMATION

Distance: 15 km (9.37 miles) circular route.

Map: OS Landranger, sheet 58.

Start and finish: Car park which is bounded by Parkway B908 and Tullibody Road B9096 (Close to the Ring Road).

Terrain: Undulating, but without steep hills. It is not difficult.

Refreshments: Places in Alloa, the Mill Trail Visitor Centre, Alva and the Farriers Hotel at the Ochil Hills Woodlands Park, Alva.

Alloa Tower.

Coats of Arms of the 45 baronets awarded by Charles I.

financial backing of the scheme, and their Coats of Arms can be seen in the Nova Scotia Commemoration room within the castle.

Back to the route: turn right, at the T-junction already referred to, into Long Row and continue along this quiet narrow road. This road runs along the edge of the Ochil Hills with the crags of Craig Leith towering with awesome grandeur above. This road has an excellent surface for cycling until the first junction at 1.5 km where it deteriorates for a similar distance before reverting back, once again, to a good surface.

Now in Alva carry on past the sign to Alva Glen (turn right here to visit Mill Trail Visitor Centre, Alva) where the road begins to climb steeply for a short distance. At the top of the hill the road passes the old cemetery from whence it descends back down to the junction with the A91 once again. At this point it is worth noting that there is a parallel junction immediately to the east being the access road to the Ochil Hills Woodlands Park. Sharing the building with the Farriers Hotel which was once Alva House is the Visitor Centre. From here it is possible to cycle on to Tillicoultry along its wooded paths.

At the junction with the A91 carry straight across this road, and continue along this flat road for 2 km to where Devon Leisure Park and Equestrian

Centre is situated on the left. Within this centre is the Devon Colliery Engine House with its large beam engine. As with the majority of coal mines in Scotland, Devon Colliery has been closed for some time. The Engine House has been preserved as a museum which is well worth a visit, although it is seldom open at weekends.

On now to the T-junction with the B9140 where a left turn is made. Follow this road for a matter of 25 m or so to the beginning of Fishcross, just long enough to cross the bridge over a disused railway. At the other side of this bridge, turn left again following this narrow road between the railway embankment and three semi-detached houses. After this, cross over another bridge and follow the track as it descends to the pathway beneath. This pathway formed along the route of the dismantled Alloa to Kinross railway is now part of the Devon Way which forms an 11 km.off-road path linking Alloa, Sauchie, Tillicoultry and Dollar. (There is also an access road on to the Devon Way from the Devon Leisure Park.)

Turn right on to this path way and head along it for 1.5 km to Main Street, New Sauchie at the Bridge Cafe. (The Devon Way continues into Alloa. However I do not think that it is particularly suitable for cycling.) Turn right on to Main Street and continue to the junction with Fairfield Road turning right again. From here take the first on the left which is Parkhead Road (B908). This junction is signposted College. Continue on this road for another kilometre back to the car park from where the route began.

Looking over Alva with the Ochil hills behind.

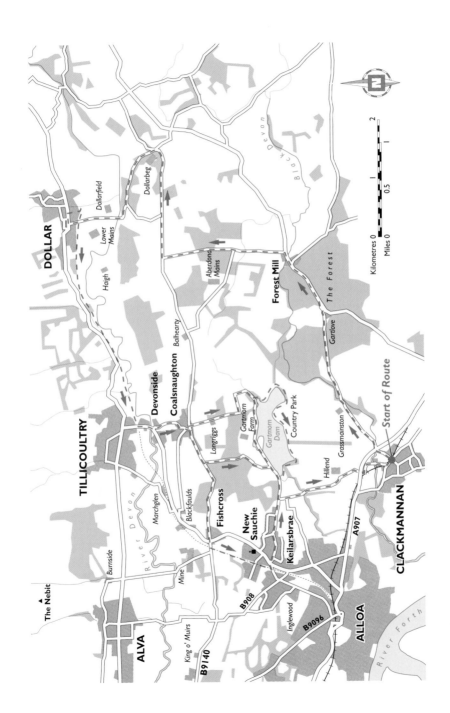

CLACKMANNAN TO DOLLAR

This route guide only takes the briefest look at the area for there is so much to see and describe that it could comprise a book of its own. Clackmannan was made a Royal Burgh by King William the Lion. The area was in the hands of the Earls of Annandale who were part of the Bruce family and it is believed that King David II who was the son of King Robert I (Robert the Bruce) lived in the castle at Clackmannan for a time. It is not known what happened to this castle but it is likely to have been replaced by the present tower in the fourteenth century for around it there are signs of earlier buildings.

The Clack Mannan (the stone of Mannan) can be seen seated on a high plinth at the Town Cross next to the Tollbooth and the Mercat Cross. Mannan was the name of the Celtic Sea God and is also the basis of the names of Slamannan, Dalmeny and the Isle of Man. According to legend the stone originally lay at the foot of a ridge at the edge of a loch, in an area to the south of the village, known as Lookaboutye and was moved into the village by Robert the Bruce.

The route begins outside the Tollbooth in Main Street. Commence along this road in an easterly direction, past the Library gifted by Andrew Carnagie, to the junction with Alloa Road. Carry straight on over this junction to the B910 signposted for Kinross. Go under the A907 after which the road begins to climb, slowly at first and then becoming steeper, for 3 km, taking you to the junction with the A977. Turn left.

Take care on this busy road, the route follows it uphill into Forest Mill. At Forest Mill there is a Pottery and Coffee shop which is worth a visit particularly after the exertion of the previous 3 km. Take the first turning on the left signposted for Aberdona and Coalsnaughton and continue uphill

INFORMATION

Distance: 22 km (13.75 miles) circular route.

Map: OS Landranger, sheet 58.

Start and finish: There are no public car parks in Clackmannan the route therefore begins outside the Town Hall in Main Street.

Terrain: Very hilly in places, with prolonged uphill stretches between Clackmannan and Dollar, particularly within the first two miles. Almost half of the route is off-road track all of which is a registered right of way, with no prohibition on cycling. However, please follow the country code, close all gates, and dismount if you come across any farm animals to avoid startling them. There are one or two locations, over short distances where I recommend that you should dismount and walk.

Refreshments: Places in Clackmannan, Dollar, Tillicoultry, Coalsnaughton and the Pottery at Forest Mill.

The wild fowl of Gartmorn Reservoir.

steeply for a short distance before having the relief of the first downhill stretch. Carry along this road between extensive woodland and ignoring the sign for Aberdona continue to its end at the B9140. Here turn right follow-ing the signs for Dollar. Carry along this flat road for 2.25 km to the junction with the B913, past Dollarbeg and continue in the direction of Dollar.

The road now begins to descend into the beautiful Devon Valley where the picturesque village of Dollar is situated. Ponder awhile at the top of this hill, for the view over the village with Castle Campbell at the top of Dollar Glen, all set within the backdrop of the Ochil Hills, is breathtaking. Enter the village through Devon Road and turn right into Bridge Street.

Dollar is well worth taking some time to explore. If however, it is your intention to visit Castle Campbell I recommend you leave your bicycle in the village and climb through Dollar Glen on foot for the inclines are severe. Visit also Dollar Museum with its fine exhibition of local history.

Leave Dollar by way of Station Road, at the end of which is the track bed of the Alloa to Kinross Railway, closed in the early 1960s. This route is another part of the Devon Way. Carry along this pleasant off-road route for 4 km to where it joins the A908 in Tillicoultry.

Tillicoultry, is one of the Hill Foot Villages and as with the others in the area, such as Alva and Menstrie is renowned for the production of woollen garments. It is on the Mill Trail which offers a unique insight into the historical development of this industry and the production of traditional Scottish woollen materials such as tartan and tweed. The local mill is Clock Mill where visitors are welcome.

Turn left on to the A908 and follow this road for a very short distance, over the River Devon and turn left again, immediately after the river bridge, on to a minor road signposted for Coalsnaughton. Commence up this steep hill for half a kilometre.to where the road begins to level off. At this point the small village of Coalsnaughton is reached. There are several hostelries at the top of this hill so if one gets too tired, rest and sustenance can be easily acquired. Soon the T-junction with the B9140 is reached where three ways back to Clackmannan are now possible.

First: Turn left on to the B9140 and then within a few metres take the first road on the right. Commence down this road which very quickly becomes a track and follow it to the north eastern end of the Gartmorn Dam, the oldest manmade reservoir in Scotland built in 1713, part of Gartmorn Country Park, where there is a surfaced footpath all the way round. Head west either on the northside or southside footpath. Once at the west end of the dam, where the visitor centre is located, the three routes once again merge.

Second: Turn right on to the B9140 and carry along it towards Fishcross for almost one kilometre to where a signed public footpath is located on the left of the road. There is also a sign for Gartmornhill Farm. Carry along this track to where the junction with the farm access road is located and turn right. Continue uphill quite steeply for a short distance to where a 3 m high tree stump is found. Here the track peters out and I recommend that the remaining 500 m to Gartmorn Dam along a rough downhill path, which can be muddy, be done on foot. At the end of this path there is a stock gate after which the dam's perimeter track is found. Here turn left and follow this track through a car park to a junction from where the visitor centre is located by turning left.

Third: Turn right on to the B9140 and carry along it to Fishcross. Carry straight on at the four-way junction for less than 100 m and turn right onto the path joining the Devon Way, described in full at the end of the last route. Turn right on to the Devon Way and head along it for 1.5 km to Main Street, New Sauchie at the Bridge Cafe. Turn left and within a few metres turn left again on to the A908 only to leave it again immediately by turning right into Shaw Court signposted to Gartmorn Country Park. Once on Shaw Court take care at the road humps, which are located every 100 metres along its length, carry along this road for a kilometre into the park. Just after the entrance to the park a public footpath to Clackmannan is located.

Gartmorn Country Park Visitor Centre is well worth a visit with plenty of information about the park much of it in the form of leaflets. There is also a good children's section. Cycle parking is available outside the centre.

Gartmore dam, near Clackmannan.

From the centre turn west and follow the road almost 500 m. past the junction at the car park to where a T-junction is reached. Turn left here and follow the sign indicating Public Footpath to Clackmannan 2 km. After a short distance the road sweeps round to the left and a track carries straight on. Looking back you can see, to the north the Ochil Hills to the west the Campsie Hills and to the south Alloa and the Forth Valley through to Grangemouth with its industrial smoke trail. From here, there is also the first glimpse of the Clackmannan Tower ahead as you ride. Take this narrow track, which is quite muddy in places, along past another route marked by way markers and a kissing gate at either side of the track. Carry on over a small rise, after which the track broadens out significantly as it passes close to Hillend Farm. From this point the village of Clackmannan is clearly visible. Soon the track passes the farm access road and continues under a railway bridge and on a few metres further to the A907.

Just before the junction with the main road there is a small unmade access road on the left. Take this to the next opening on to the main road. This negates having to ride along this busy main road for the route continues directly on the other side of the A907. Cross the main road then and continue straight along the minor road, known as Mill Road. Pass the turning signposted for Helensfield, over the bridge spanning the Black Devon, and into a new (at the time of writing) housing estate. From here turn right and continue uphill for a few metres, then turning right again out of this estate on to an old road, with a white semi-detached house on it (one half of which is called Mill Villa). Commence uphill and on to the road junction with Alloa Road and turning left. Follow this road for a few metres to the first turning on the right which is Cattle Market. This leads directly into Main Street where the route began.

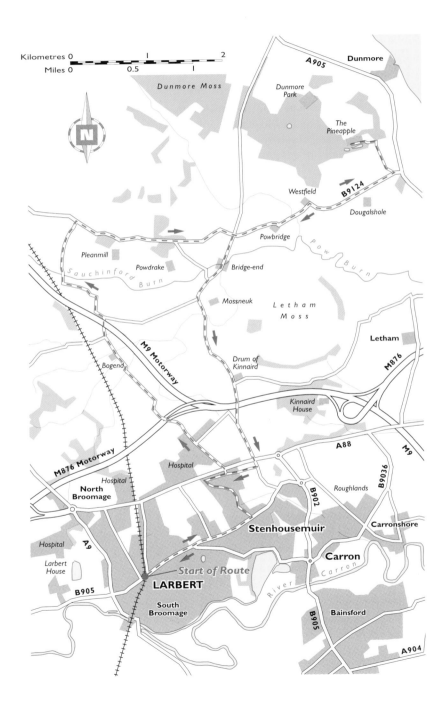

LARBERT TO THE PINEAPPLE

The name Larbert is derived from the Celtic term Lar-Beart meaning Field of Action which is truly a testament to this area, particularly in Roman times where the close proximity of the Roman Empire's most remote border and the fierce and warlike demeanour of the tribes who lived to the north guaranteed many a military action.

This area is most well-known for its Iron Founding industry. However, as every Scottish child will tell you the most popular product to come from there is McCowan's Toffee either in bars or as penny dainties. The latter, when I was a boy, were so large they barely fitted into a child's mouth.

The route begins at Larbert Railway Station. Leave the station and commence north-east along Main Street for 1.25 km passing into Stenhousemuir where the name of the street changes to King Street. Stenhousemuir is the home of the 'Warriors' which is the local name for the senior football club which takes its official name from the town.

Turn left into Muirhead Road and carry along as it meanders through Antonshill Housing Estate. Eventually it turns through 90 degrees to continue as Edward Avenue. Take the first street on the left, which is Hamilton Avenue, then travel the short distance to the T-junction with Bellsdyke Road. Dismount and cross this junction which is blocked to traffic and then commence across Bellsdyke Road and leading into Hamilton Road.

INFORMATION

Distance: 22 km (13.75) circular route.

Map: OS Landranger, sheet 65.

Start and finish: Larbert Railway Station.

Terrain: Almost completely flat. It is not difficult.

Refreshments: Many places in Larbert.

Plean Tower.

Continue along Hamilton Road past Bellsdyke Hospital and over the M876 Motorway and continue for 1.25 km,turning first left at the junction and then passing under the M9 Motorway, to the next junction.

On reaching this junction turn left and follow the minor road as it makes a number of right angle turns before passing a most imposing building with the flag of St.Andrew proudly flying over its tower. This is Plean Tower, recently restored to reflect its former glory as a fifteenth century baronial hall.

Soon after the castle aT-junction is reached. Here turn right on to the B9124 signposted for Airth. Carry along this road for 5 km. to within a few metres of the A905. Turn left at a sign for East Lodge and enter Dunmore Park where the Pineapple is located. Carry along the estate road to the car park (please note there is no cycle parking at this location) adjacent to the walled garden within which the Pineapple forms an imposing focal point.

The Pineapple which was built in 1761 as a garden retreat, is a two-storey building with a high domed roof in the shape of a perfect pineapple. It was gifted by the Countess of Perth to the National Trust for Scotland in 1974. At this time it was completely renovated and can be rented out as holiday accommodation. It is reckoned, by some, to be Scotland's most bizarre building.

Leave by the same route out of the estate and double back along the B9124 already travelled, to the four-way junction some two kilometres further on. Here the route turns south by making a left turn, however if you look into the adjacent field to the north, you may catch a glimpse of a strange herd for Scotland, that of ostriches. Please heed the warning signs on the fences because these birds can be very dangerous, their long necks allowing them to get their beaks a considerable distance over the fence.

After turning to the left continue down this minor road for a kilometre to the next junction where a left turn is made. Follow this flat road past Letham Moss and spanning the M9 once more before continuing on to the junction with the A88 once again. Here cross this road and commence up the short pathway connecting to Edward Avenue and turn right. Retrace the route back to Larbert Railway Station via Edward Avenue, Muirhead Road, King Street and Main Street.

The Pineapple.

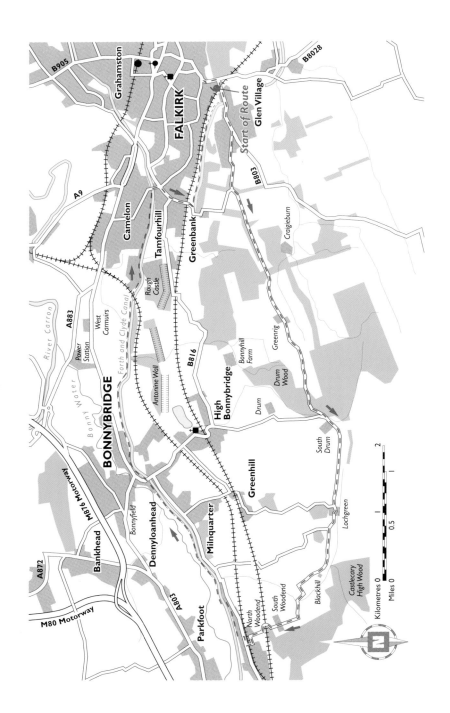

FALKIRK TO BONNYBRIDGE VIA ALLANDALE

Falkirk or Fawe Kirk meaning the speckled Church, is a Burgh, and has been one since 1600. However it has been in existence for many centuries before this, and has had more than its fair share in events that have shaped Scotland's history. Starting from Roman times it was the site of a fort; the location of which was not discovered until 1990. It was also the name given to two famous battles, although the actual geographical locations of these could hardly be said to be in Falkirk itself.

The first battle was in 1298 when William Wallace's forces fought the biggest English army to be assembled thus far in Scotland: consisting of 25,000 infantry and almost 6,000 cavalry under Edward I (The Hammer of the Scots, so called). The Scottish forces were not united, for most of the noble men fighting at Wallace's side were on the one hand part of Norman families, therefore having lands in England. On the other hand many of them were jealous of Wallace in his position as guardian of Scotland because he was a commoner. Midway through the battle these knights deserted the scene leaving the English no difficulty in defeating the Scots. After the battle was over many of the fleeing Scottish knights went to Edward to plead

INFORMATION

Distance: 19 km (11.87 miles) circular route.

Map: OS Landranger, sheet 65.

Start and finish: Falkirk High Railway Station.

Terrain: this route is undulating but without steep hills. It is not difficult.

Refreshments: Many places in Falkirk in Bonnybridge, and the Underwood Lockhouse on the Forth and Clyde Canal.

The Antonine Wall at Seabegs wood.

forgiveness. One of these was Bruce who, within a very few years would defeat the English – at Bannockburn – and re-establish Scotland's independence. The graves of many of the Scottish dead can still be seen in the old church yard in Falkirk.

The outcome of the two battles of Falkirk could not be more different, for in the first, the battle was a defeat for Scotland, but later the final struggle was to see Scotland the victor. The second was a victory in battle, whilst just over two months later, the cause was finally defeated.

The second battle of Falkirk was in January 1746, between the forces of the Government and the Jacobites, under Prince Charles Edward Stuart (Bonnie Prince Charlie) ending in victory for the Jacobites.

Falkirk became famous for the Tryst, which was the national meeting place for the sale of farm animals and was the gathering place for drovers and dealers from all parts of the Western Isles and Ross-shire in the North to Yorkshire in the South. The Tryst took place on the second Tuesday of August, September and October. Today the Tryst is limited to a weekend, and shares the venue with the Fair.

In the eighteenth and the nineteenth centuries Falkirk was the centre of the Iron Industry in Scotland, due to the plentiful supply of iron ore being mined in the district. One notable company was the Carron Iron Company who were one of the first to exploit the canal as a means of transporting their products.

Today Falkirk is a fine town, mixing the modern with the traditional. Most of the industry in the area is confined to Grangemouth and other surrounding areas.

The route begins at Falkirk High Railway Station which has four cycle parking stands to accommodate eight bikes comfortably. Commence down High Station Road for 250 m and turn right at a petrol station building into Glen Brae. Carry on up this steep hill to the Slamannan Road (B803) 200 m farther on the right. Take this road over the railway and still climbing steeply carry on for a kilometre to the Y-junction with Lochgreen Road. Commence along it, as it takes a much flatter course. After leaving the town the road passes the Bantaskin Estate which is open to the public. This is where the second battle of Falkirk was fought in 1746. This undulating road continues for almost 5 km to a junction. From here a right turn takes a route to High Bonnybridge from where the canal can be reached.

The route which veers to the left continues west along the high ground passing pleasant farmland. One of the farms is Lochgreen after which the road takes its name. Pass the next three junctions before descending into the small village of Allandale. Take care on this 2 km descent for there are a few difficult turns to be negotiated before the village is reached on the B816. It may be interesting to note that this is another area where the route to the west is described in 25 Cycle Routes in and around Glasgow. On reaching the B816, turn right and continue for 500 m, passing through Allandale with its interesting cottage terraces, to Underwood Lockhouse from where there is access to the Forth and Clyde Canal.

On reaching the canal commence along the tow path in an easterly direction towards Falkirk retracing the latter part of the route outlined in Route 11, until Bonnybridge is reached. At this point merely continue along the tow path to the present end of the Forth and Clyde Canal at the Union Inn in Falkirk.

The route passes Bonnybridge a small mining, and foundry town, from where access to another Roman Fort can be reached. This is Rough Castle situated about 10 minutes cycling from the canal, and its location is clearly signposted. Access is along a farm road, then via a rough track to a car park. Along this track lies Bonnybridge House, and between this point, and Rough Castle itself lies the best preserved section of the Antonine Wall, with rampart and ditch, the remains of two signalling platforms, and even traces of the military way can be seen.

Back to the canal, as it crosses the B816 at Bonnybridge,you should look out for a colourful mural on the exterior walls of the foundry by the bridge over the canal.

Underwood Lockhouse
on the Forth/Clyde canal.

Three miles on brings us to Falkirk via Camelon. Today the Forth and Clyde Canal finishes its 35-mile journey from Bowling, in Falkirk with the last few miles to the River Forth being culverted, but before it finishes it descends through a picturesque series of locks starting at lock 16. Opposite these locks is the Union Inn. It was here that the Forth and Clyde Canal was linked by a series of locks to the Union Canal at Greenbank.

The Union Canal was opened in 1822 and enjoyed brief but considerable popularity as a means of transport with as many as 200,000 people using it in 1836.

However, the Glasgow to Edinburgh Railway was opened in 1842 and with this faster mode of transportation the popularity of the canal dwindled very quickly. However, thanks to its beautiful surroundings, for some further considerable time it was enjoyed by many people as a leisure activity with pleasure boats plying its length.

Once the traveller has left the Forth and Clyde Canal the way is still open today to continue the journey to Edinburgh along the tow path of the Union Canal.

The junction of the two canals was known as Port Downie and it was here that the two canals were joined together by a series of eleven locks ascending 110 feet in less than a kilometre. These locks were closed in 1933 and were subsequently filled in. Today the Union Inn is still a place for some refreshment before the traveller continues the journey to Edinburgh along the Union Canal.

Union canal tunnel

After leaving the Inn turn right and quickly right again on to Glenfuir Road. This soon becomes Greenbank Road and winds its way uphill to where the Union Canal is situated a quarter of a mile further on.

Once on the tow path of the Union Canal it is approximately one and a half kilometres back to Falkirk High Station via South Bantaskin Road. Turn right into Gartcows Road, at the end of which it joins High Station Road. At the top of this road Falkirk High Station is reached.

INDEX

The Stationery Office

Published by The Stationery Office and available from:

The Stationery Office Bookshops
71 Lothian Road, Edinburgh EH3 9AZ
(counter service only)
49 High Holborn, London WC1V 6HB
(counter service and fax orders only)
Fax 0171-831 1326
68-69 Bull Street, Birmingham B4 6AD
0121-236 9696 Fax 0121-236 9699
33 Wine Street, Bristol BS1 2BQ
0117-926 4306 Fax 0117-929 4515
9-21 Princess Street, Manchester M60 8AS
0161-834 7201 Fax 0161-833 0634
16 Arthur Street, Belfast BT1 4GD
01232 238451 Fax 01232 235401
The Stationery Office Oriel Bookshop
The Friary, Cardiff CF1 4AA
01222 395548 Fax 01222 384347

The Stationery Office publications are also available from:

The Publications Centre
(mail, telephone and fax orders only)
PO Box 276, London SW8 5DT
General enquiries 0171-873 0011
Telephone orders 0171-873 9090
Fax orders 0171-873 8200

Accredited Agents
(see Yellow Pages)

and through good booksellers